COLLINS
SCHOOL
GRAMMAR

JOHN MANNION

Head of English, Elliot School

Collins Educational

Published by Collins Educational
An imprint of HarperCollins*Publishers* Ltd
77–85 Fulham Palace Road
London W6 8JB

First published 1998

ISBN 000 322 116 4

British Library Cataloguing in Publication Data
A catalogue record for this book is available from the British Library.

Commissioned by Domenica de Rosa

Project management by Lisa English

Edited by Kim Richardson

Cover and internal design by Nigel Jordan

Cover illustration © Tony Stone

Illustrations by Clinton Banbury and Harry Venning

Production by Susan Cashin

Printed and bound by Scotprint Ltd, Musselburgh

To Kate, Joe, Pat and Jess – my favourite list of proper nouns.

A, an

'A' and 'an' (sometimes called 'the indefinite article') are used before singular nouns, usually to convey a general meaning.

 I'll buy you a present.
He made a mistake.

In the examples above, it is not specified what present will be bought, or what mistake was made.

When to use 'a' and 'an'
- 'A' is used before nouns that start with consonants (all the letters in the alphabet except vowels).
- 'An' is used before nouns that start with vowels (a, e, i, o, u).
- 'Some' is used when nouns are in the plural.

 She ate a curry.
He cooked an excellent curry.
Some curries are too hot for me.

Sometimes 'a' is used before nouns that start with a consonant sound, and 'an' is used before nouns that start with a vowel sound.

 She captured a unicorn.
We booked into an hotel.

Which nouns?
'A' and 'an' can only be used in front of countable nouns.

 an apple, a banana, a carrot
but not a rice, a money, a water

Using 'a' and 'an'
'A', 'an', 'some' and 'the' ('the' is also called 'the definite article') can be used to test if a word is a noun. If a word makes sense when it has 'a', 'an', 'some' or 'the' in front of it, then it is working as a noun.

 a car, an elephant, some toys, the palace

Even words that are usually thought of as adjectives or verbs can work like nouns when they are used with 'a', 'an', 'some' and 'the'.

 a green, the run, some fat

 Speaking and listening activity

Brainstorm more adjectives and verbs that can work like nouns when they are used with 'a', 'an', 'some' and 'the'.

Look up

Adjective, Article, Countable noun, Noun, Plural, Singular, The, Verb.

Abstract noun

Abstract nouns are a type of noun that describes qualities, states or ideas. They refer to things that you cannot see, hear, taste, touch or smell. They therefore contrast with concrete nouns.

Countable and uncountable
Many abstract nouns are uncountable.

 advice, fun, luck, courage

However, some abstract nouns have both uncountable and countable usages.

 Argument never got anyone anywhere. (uncountable)
That isn't a good *argument*. (countable)

Opposites
Abstract nouns can often have opposites.

 love/hate, courage/cowardice, reality/fantasy

Using abstract nouns

In writing, abstract nouns can often be used to create vague general impressions. They are common in advertising copy.

 shock, terror, heartache

Reading activity

You can see how abstract nouns work by comparing two First World War poems – Rupert Brooks' 'The Soldier' and Wilfred Owen's 'Dulce et Decorum Est'. Find all the abstract nouns in Brooks' poem, and all the concrete nouns in Owen's poem. What different impressions do the poems give?

 Look up

Concrete noun, Countable noun, Noun, Uncountable noun.

Accent

Accent refers to the way in which words are pronounced.

Different accents

Accent is not connected to the grammar of what is said, but is determined by such things as where people were born, where they live now, their education or their social class.

It is possible to speak perfectly correct Standard English with a local accent (e.g. a Yorkshire accent), a class accent (e.g. a posh accent) or a national accent (e.g. an American accent).

5

Look up
Dialect.

Active voice

The voice of a verb can be either active or passive. When a verb is in the active voice the subject of the sentence is usually the person or thing that performs the action. The subject comes before the verb.

 The bus will arrive soon.
Joanne ran the marathon.

Verbs that always use the active voice
Some verbs always use the active voice.

 rise, blush, disappear

Using the active voice

Writing that uses verbs in the active voice is usually more direct and immediate than writing that uses the passive voice. For instance, in the sentence

The ball was passed to Southgate

we cannot tell who passed the ball. We would have to add an extra phrase such as 'by the goalkeeper' if we wished to include this information. Compare:

The goalkeeper passed the ball to Southgate.

Look up
Passive voice, Subject, Verb.

Adjective

Adjectives are words that give information about nouns.

Where do they go?
Adjectives usually go in front of the noun they describe, but they can follow verbs like 'be' or 'appear'.

He aimed at the *small* target.
The target is *small*.

Grading and comparing

Adjectives can often be graded and compared.

 The balloon is *large*.
That balloon is *very large*.
This balloon is *larger* than that one.
That is the *largest* balloon.

large   larger   largest

When verbs and nouns work like adjectives

As with many other traditional 'parts of speech', adjectives are not defined by type but by how they are used in a sentence. 'Red', for example, is usually thought of as an adjective, but the word 'red' can also be used as a noun ('the colour red'). In the same way, other words which might be thought of as 'verbs' or 'nouns' can have adjectival functions.

 the *running* water
the *village* green

In the second example above, 'village' is acting as an adjective, and 'green' is acting as a noun!

A
B
C
D
E
F
G
H
I
J
K
L
M
N
O
P
Q
R
S
T
U
V
W
X
Y
Z

Using adjectives

Adjectives are important in all areas of writing. The choice of adjective helps to create atmosphere, tone and mood: this is especially important in writing fiction and poetry.

 Reading activity

Look at the advertisements in a colour magazine and list all the adjectives used. What kind of tone or mood do they create?

Look up

Comparative, Noun, Superlative.

Adjunct

An adjunct is a part of the clause that tells you something about the circumstances of an action, event or situation. Adjuncts are either adverbs or prepositional phrases. They are sometimes referred to as adverbials.

What adjuncts tell you

Adjuncts indicate the time or place of an action or event, its frequency or the manner in which it occurs.

 The fête opened *at 2 o'clock*.
Every Saturday, Charmaine helped in the shop.
William wrote *rapidly*.

Look up

Adverb, Adverbial, Clause, Preposition.

Adverb

An adverb is a word or phrase that tells you more about the verb. It can also tell you about the whole of a sentence or clause.

 Leon spoke *quietly*.
Faye did all of her work *thoughtfully*.

What adverbs tell you about actions

Adverbs can tell you how, when and where actions happened.

 fitfully, quietly, smoothly   *Adverbs of manner (how)*
now, yesterday, tomorrow   *Adverbs of time (when)*
here, there, everywhere   *Adverbs of place (where)*

Grading and comparing adverbs

Adverbs of manner can be graded and compared.

 Neris walked *more quickly* than Cibelly.
Graham complained *most loudly*.

The degree of an adverb can be shown by words like 'quite', 'very', 'completely', 'extremely' and 'fairly'.

Where do they go?

Adverbs are often placed next to the verb, but many adverbs can occur at almost any point in a sentence or clause.

 Tim walked *slowly* home.
Tim walked home *slowly*.
Slowly, Tim walked home.

Using adverbs

Adverbs have a wide variety of uses. You can use them to make your writing or speech more precise by answering the questions 'How?', 'When?' and 'Where?'

 Look up

Comparative, Superlative, Verb.

Adverbial

An adverbial is a word, phrase or clause that tells us more about the way in which an action happened, or why it happened. It is another term for adjunct. Adverbials are adverbs or prepositional phrases.

 The train arrived *noisily*.
The train arrived *on time*.
The train arrived *at three in the morning*.
After some delay the train arrived.
Though no one expected it, the train arrived.

9

Look up
Adjunct, Adverb, Preposition.

Affix

An affix is a general term for a part of a word added onto another. When added to the beginning of a word it is known as a prefix, and when added to the end of a word it is known as a suffix.

Using affixes

Prefixes and suffixes make English very flexible, so that even relatively new words like 'hassle' can be quickly fitted into the language and given a range of meanings and uses, such as 'hassling', 'unhassled' and 'hassle-free'.

Reading activity

In George Orwell's novel *1984* a new version of English, called Newspeak, is proposed. Its intention is to restrict thought rather than to enlarge it, but the new language makes extensive use of affixes. Instead of having two words 'good' and 'bad', Newspeak has one word 'good', and the idea of bad is expressed by 'ungood'. Very bad is 'plusungood' and badly is 'ungoodful'. Read 'The Principles of Newspeak', the Appendix to *1984*.

Writing activity

Now try inventing some Newspeak terms of your own.

Look up
Prefix, Suffix, Word origins.

Agreement

Agreement is a relationship between different parts of a sentence.

Subject–verb agreement
Subject–verb agreement means that singular subjects are used with singular verb forms and plural subjects have plural verb

forms. In practice, this mainly relates to the third person form of regular verbs since this is the only one that changes.

 I *open* the door.   *First person singular*
Patrick *opens* the door.   *Third person singular*
We *open* the door.   *First person plural*

Subject–verb agreement also applies to irregular verbs such as 'be'.

 I *am*
You *are*
He/she/it *is*
We/you/they *are*.

Gender agreement

Gender agreement is also necessary.

 Susan was annoyed with *herself*.
Brian sold *his* bike.

Beware long sentences!

Agreement causes few problems in short sentences, but in longer sentences, where there is a gap between the subject and its verb, confusion can occur. In the sentence below, the subject – 'everyone' – is in the third person singular and should take 'is', not 'are'.

 Everyone, whether in the lower school or the upper school, and whether taking exams or not, are expected to attend Speech Day.

None

'None' can also cause problems. It stands for 'no one' and requires a singular verb (just as 'one' does). To help you remember this, think of 'none' as standing for 'not one'.

 Of all the cakes in the competition none *is* better than this one.

None of the boys who were here last week *has* arrived today.

Collective nouns and agreement

When collective nouns are used, such as 'class' or 'committee', it can be difficult to decide if they are singular or plural. 'The class' is one thing, but it is made up of several people, so should we say 'The class is …' or 'The class are …'? Generally 'is' is used when the class as a whole is being referred to, and 'are' is used when the individual members of the class are being referred to.

 The class is meeting at lunchtime.   (*the whole of it*)
The class are discussing it.   (*the individual members*)

Note that singular verbs must not be used with plural pronouns, and vice versa.

 The class *is* waiting for *its* teacher.
not The class *is* waiting for *their* teacher.
or The class *are* waiting for *its* teacher.

Look up

Collective noun, Gender, Person, Plural, Singular, Subject, Verb.

An

See A, an.

Anglo-Saxon

See English.

Apostrophe

The apostrophe is a punctuation mark which looks like this **'**. It is used to show either possession or a missing letter. In grammatical terms the apostrophe is an example of an inflection.

How apostrophes show possession
If the noun is singular, you add an apostrophe and an 's' to show possession.

> **Eg.** Ian's bike
> The bird's wing

If the noun is plural and ends in 's', you just add an apostrophe after the 's'.

> **Eg.** The fishes' gills
> The girls' books

If the noun is plural and does not end in 's', you add an apostrophe and an 's'.

> **Eg.** The men's coats
> The children's party

Charles's or Charles'?
Most proper nouns ending in 's' can either end in an apostrophe or can add an extra 's' after the apostrophe.

> **Eg.** Dickens' novels *or* Dickens's novels
> Keats' poetry *or* Keats's poetry

If it is difficult to pronounce the extra 's', then you usually omit it.

> **Eg.** Moses' anger *not* Moses's anger

Shop and street names
Many shop and street names should have an apostrophe, but this is often missed out by sign writers and logo designers.

> **Eg.** Woolworths, Boots, Kings Lane

Woolworths and Boots should be written Woolworth's and Boot's, as they stand for 'Woolworth's shop' and 'Boot's shop'. Likewise, there is an apostrophe in the following general shop names.

> **Eg.** Go to the chemist's, will you? (= *chemist's shop*)
> Jones' is the best butcher's. (= *butcher's shop*)

Jones' is the best butcher's

Decades and centuries

Watch out for references to decades and centuries such as 'the 1950s' and 'the 1800s'. As they are actually plurals, not possessives, they should not be written with an apostrophe.

 In the 1990s ... *not* In the 1990's ...

Its or it's?

Another source of confusion is the possessive determiner 'its'. Many people think that because apostrophes indicate possession, the possessive pronoun 'its' should have an apostrophe. This is not the case.

 The dog ate its dinner.
Its wings are easily damaged.

When 'it's' has an apostrophe, it is a shortened form of 'it is' (see below).

How apostrophes show missing letters

The other use of the apostrophe is to show where a letter or letters have been missed out of a word.

It's raining again today.   (*it's = it is*)
I can't go out tonight.   (*can't = cannot*)
He might've been killed.   (*might've = might have*)
The wave crashed over the   (*fo'c's'le = forecastle*)
    fo'c's'le and soaked the first mate.
''Ave you 'anded in your 'omework?' asked Harry.

Inflection, Plural, Possessive determiner, Proper noun, Singular.

Article

Articles come before nouns. 'A', 'an' and 'some', which are known as indefinite articles, tell us about unspecified nouns. 'The' is known as the definite article and refers to a particular noun.

 The thief stole a valuable picture.
The thief stole the most valuable picture in the gallery.

Look up

A, Noun, The.

Auxiliary verb

Auxiliary verbs are verbs such as 'be', 'have' and 'do' which help in the formation of tenses or questions.

'Be' as an auxiliary verb
The verb 'be' helps to form continuous tenses in which '-ing' is added to the base form of a regular verb.

 I *am* going   (*continuous present*)
I *was* going   (*continuous past*)
I will *be* going   (*continuous future*)

'Have' as an auxiliary verb
The verb 'have' helps to form perfect tenses in which '-ed' is added to the base form of a regular verb.

I *have* waited   (*present perfect*)
I *had* waited   (*past perfect*)
I will *have* waited   (*future perfect*)

'Have' and 'be' can be used in combination with another verb to form perfect continuous tenses.

 You *have been* listening   (*present perfect continuous*)
You *had been* listening   (*past perfect continuous*)
You will *have been* listening (*future perfect continuous*)

'Do' as an auxiliary verb

- 'Do' helps to form questions.

  Do you want a coffee?
  When did Khalid arrive?
  You like chocolate, don't you?

- 'Do' makes positive statements and commands more forceful.

  I do think he was rude!
  Do be quiet!

- 'Do' also helps to form negative statements and commands. In speech or in informal writing it is usually shortened to 'doesn't' or 'don't'.

  He does not live here any more.
  Don't touch that!

- 'Do' can be used to replace a verb or verb phrase used earlier in a sentence in order to avoid repetition.

  You look as pretty as Carla does.   (= *as pretty as Carla looks*)

Look up

Base form, Be, Directive, Do, Have, Informal language, Tense, Verb.

Back formation

See Word origins.

Base form

The base form is the part of a verb that '-ed', '-ing' and other endings are added to.

> **Eg** want, talk, work

Adding to the base form

- The base form + 's' forms the third person singular.

  > **Eg** he walks, she blames, it moves

- 'To' + the base form is called the infinitive.

  > **Eg** to walk, to blame, to move

- The base form + 'ing' forms the present participle.

  > **Eg** walking, blaming, moving

- The base form + 'ed' forms the past participle.

  > **Eg** walked, blamed, moved

Commands

The base form is always used in commands.

> **Eg** Listen!, Be quiet!, Have fun!

The base form in irregular verbs

In many irregular verbs the spelling of the base form is not preserved in all tenses.

base form	past tense	past participle
freeze	froze	frozen
do	did	done
eat	ate	eaten
go	went	gone

A B C D E F G H I J K L M N O P Q R S T U V W X Y Z

 Look up

Directive, Infinitive, Participle, Verb.

Be

The verb 'be' is not only a common verb in its own right: it also plays an important part in the formation of verb tenses.

The forms of 'be'

'Be' is highly irregular. The simple forms of 'be' are:

Present	Past
I *am*	I *was*
you *are*	you *were*
she/he/it *is*	she/he/it *was*
we *are*	we *were*
you *are*	you *were*
they *are*	they *were*

How 'be' forms verb tenses

As an auxiliary verb 'be' helps to form several tenses of other verbs.

Eg. She *is* waiting.   (*continuous present tense*)
They *were* hoping.   (*continuous past tense*)
I have *been* running.   (*continuous present perfect tense*)
We had *been* walking.   (*continuous past perfect tense*)
You will *be* leaving.   (*continuous future tense*)
They will have *been*   (*continuous future perfect tense*)
driving for three hours.

Other uses of 'be'

A major function of 'be' is to help form the passive voice.

Eg. We *were* robbed.
He has *been* humiliated.

'Be' is also a very common copula verb, that is one that links a subject to its complement.

Eg. Picasso *was* a painter.

 Look up

Auxiliary verb, Copula verb, Irregular, Passive voice, Tense.

Blend

See Word origins.

Bracket

The bracket is a punctuation mark which looks like this **(** (open bracket) or this **)** (end bracket).

How brackets are used
Brackets are used to mark off part of a sentence. Usually the part of the sentence inside the brackets is additional information and is not essential to a complete understanding of the sentence.

 Three students (Mark, Anne and Steve) gained full marks.
NATO (the North Atlantic Treaty Organisation) is a
    major military alliance.
Pizza (in my opinion) is over-rated.
My cat (which is a Persian) has won prizes at shows.

Brackets can often be replaced by commas or dashes.

 **Look up**
Comma, Dash, Punctuation.

Clause

Clauses are the building blocks of sentences.

Subject and verb

A clause must contain a subject and a verb, although in some clauses the subject is said to be understood and is not actually included.

 Open the door!

In this special sentence, the subject ('you') is 'understood'.

Clauses in different types of sentence

- A simple sentence consists of a single clause.

   Colin shivered.
  The cat looked guilty.

- Compound and complex sentences consist of combinations of clauses.

   <u>I bought a burger</u> <u>but Jonathan chose a sandwich</u>.

  First clause   Second clause

  <u>Kelly left her house at eight o'clock</u> <u>and ran for the bus</u>.

  First clause   Second clause (subject shared)

  <u>Pamela wore formal clothes on Fridays,</u>
  <u>   although company policy was to dress casually</u>.

  Main clause   Subordinate clause

Look up

Complex sentence, Compound sentence, Main clause, Sentence, Simple sentence, Special sentence, Subject, Subordinate clause, Verb.

Clause elements

Clauses consist of a subject and a verb and three other elements: objects, complements and adverbials (or adjuncts). Clause elements can be either single words or groups of words.

Seven types of clause structure

There are only seven basic types of clause structure in English. These are:

Paula ran.
 S   V

Paula phoned the hospital.
 S   V   O

She listened carefully.
 S   V   A

Paula is a doctor.
 S   V   C

She gave me some medicine.
 S   V   O   O

Paula dropped her stethoscope on the floor.
 S   V   O   A

She got her stethoscope dirty.
 S   V   O   C

Key:	S	=	subject
	V	=	verb
	O	=	object
	A	=	adverbial
	C	=	complement

Using clause elements

The naming and identification of clause elements played a large part in traditional grammar teaching. They present few problems in short sentences, but in longer and more complicated sentences it is always useful to be able to identify elements such as the main verb and the subject. These can be checked by asking 'Who or what is this sentence about?' (that is, what is the subject?) and 'What is being done?' (that is, what is the verb?). If these two things are kept firmly in mind there is less difficulty in knowing when to use a full stop: when a new subject and a new verb are introduced, start a new sentence.

Look up

Adjunct, Adverbial, Complement, Object, Subject, Verb.

Clipping

See Word origins.

Coining

See Word origins.

Collective noun

A collective noun is the name of a group of things considered as a whole.

 school, flock, class, committee

A robbery of starlings

Singular or plural?

Collective nouns refer to more than one thing but they can be followed by either singular or plural verbs and pronouns, depending on whether the group as a whole or the individuals in the group are being referred to.

 The class *is* waiting for *its* teacher.
The class *are* putting *their* books away.

Writing activity

There are some very unusual collective nouns such as a 'charm' of goldfinches, an 'orchestra' of computers, an 'unkindness' of ravens and a 'kindle' of kittens. These can often be found in books about words (and sometimes only in books about words) and can be interesting to investigate. Another way of exploring collective nouns is by inventing new ones for groups of people or things, such as a 'greed' of stockbrokers, or a 'volume' of publishers. Think up ten more colourful and appropriate collective nouns for groups of people, animals or things.

Look up

Agreement, Noun.

Colloquial language

Colloquial language is the kind of language used in conversation. It is informal in structure and often includes slang, dialect and contracted forms of words.

Look up

Dialect, Informal language, Slang.

Colon

The colon is a punctuation mark which looks like this **:**.

Uses of the colon

The colon is used to indicated a pause in a sentence. It marks a stronger pause than a semi-colon, and is particularly used to introduce lists, explanations or, sometimes, quotations.

> **Eg.** The most important factors for success in this subject are: hard work, organisation and common sense.
> I'm sorry I didn't turn up: I missed the bus.
> The *Wasteland* by T.S. Eliot begins: 'April is the cruellest month'.

Look up

Punctuation, Semi-colon.

Comma

A comma is a punctuation mark which looks like this **,** . Commas are used to indicate pauses, and to separate words, phrases or clauses.

Indicating pauses
The comma is used to indicate a short pause in a sentence. They are not always necessary in sentences, as full stops are, and their position is often a matter of style or choice.

 In 1901, Queen Victoria died.
or In 1901 Queen Victoria died.

Separating items in a list
Commas can be used to separate items in a list. The items will consist of the same part of speech, and can be words, phrases or clauses.

 Red, blues, yellows and golds
He rushed up to the barrier, put in the ticket and ran for the train.
Running, jumping and standing still
Planets, stars, nebulas or galaxies
Quickly, slowly, heavily, lightly

Note the use of 'and' or 'or' before the last item in four of the above lists.

Commas also separate items in a string of adjectives before a noun.

 The old, worn out shoes.
Her long, neatly combed, red hair.
The pointless, stupid, squalid war.

A final 'and' is not required in such lists.

Marking off relative clauses
Commas are often used to mark off non-defining relative clauses.

 Faith, who has worked here a long time, knows her job well.
The car, which had only recently been painted, was now a complete wreck.

They should not be used, however, in defining relative clauses.

The man who lives at number 12 won on the Lottery.

Attaching information

Commas are used to attach extra information to a sentence, particularly disjuncts, conjuncts and question tags.

 The most important event in English history, in my opinion, was the Battle of Hastings.

Javier had become much more cheerful, as far as I could tell.

First of all, we need to find a bus stop.

Commas in direct speech

Commas normally introduce direct speech. When there are no question marks or exclamation marks, a comma replaces the full stop at the end of a sentence in direct speech.

 He asked, 'Can I go now?'

'I'll be with you in a minute,' he said.

Look up

Conjunct, Direct speech, Disjunct, Punctuation, Question tag, Relative clause.

Command

See Directive.

Comment

In grammar, a comment is a word, phrase or clause added to a sentence which expresses the speaker or writer's attitude.

 I think, I imagine, I'm glad to say, you see, you know

I imagine he's there by now.

How comments work

Comment clauses are often only loosely connected to the rest of the sentence in which they occur. Others are simply fillers with no particular meaning.

 William is in the kitchen, *I think*.

She's not in, *unfortunately*.

I went to the, *you know*, cinema.

Using comments

Comments are very common in speech. When they are used in writing, they help to give it a more conversational tone.

📝 Writing activity

The following paragraph is written quite formally and some people might find it too aggressive. Add comment clauses to make it less formal and less aggressive.

> Smoking should be banned. Many people find it annoying and it is bad for your health. People who smoke don't realise how unpleasant it is to be near them. It should be against the law for them to damage other people's health.

Look up

Clause, Phrase.

Common noun

A common noun is a noun that names things.

 hand, car, idea, islands, love, house, air

They're common, not proper

Common nouns are distinct from proper nouns and, except at the beginning of sentences, are not written with capital letters. Common nouns can be countable or uncountable.

Look up

Countable noun, Noun, Proper noun, Uncountable noun.

Comparative

When adjectives or adverbs are being used to compare, they can be in either the comparative or the superlative form.

Comparative adjectives

To make the comparative form of most short adjectives you add '-er'.

hot	hotter
long	longer

'More' is used with longer adjectives.

beautiful	more beautiful
childish	more childish

Comparative adverbs
'More' is used with most adverbs, whether they are long or short.

rapidly	more rapidly
often	more often

There are a few exceptions, however. The comparative of 'fast', when used both as an adjective and as an adverb, is 'faster'.

Irregular comparison
Some words have irregular comparative and superlative forms.

	Comparative	**Superlative**
good	better	best
bad	worse	worst
many	more	most
little	less	least

⌐Look up

Adjective, Adverb, Superlative.

Complement

A complement is a clause element which gives more information about the subject or object of the clause.

Sorana is *a doctor*.
He made his mother *happy*.

How complements connect
Complement elements are often connected to the subject by copula verbs such as 'be', 'seem', 'appear', etc.

Lola seems *anxious* today.

⌐Look up

Clause, Copula verb.

Complex sentence

Complex sentences are sentences that have a main clause and at least one subordinate clause.

 <u>Kate was late,</u> <u>although she had left on time</u>.

Main clause   Subordinate clause

Subordinate clauses

The subordinate clause adds extra information to the main clause and is usually connected to it by a subordinating conjunction. In the previous example, 'although' is the subordinating conjunction.

Using complex sentences

Complex sentences usually show connections and relationships and are often found in more formal writing.

 Reading activity

Look at a newspaper and compare the number of complex sentences you find in the reporting sections with those in the editorial or comment sections. What conclusions can you draw from these findings?

 Look up

Formal language, Main clause, Subordinate clause, Subordinating conjunction.

Compound sentence

Compound sentences are sentences that consist of two or more clauses joined together by conjunctions.

 Kate was late and Patrick was worried.

Leaving the second subject out

Compound sentences usually consist of two main clauses, but if the subject of both clauses is the same it is possible (and more elegant) to leave the second subject out.

 Helen won the race and Helen was given a medal *is usually written as* Helen won the race and was given a medal.

Using compound sentences

Compound sentences help to improve the flow of writing. They can also be used to achieve a powerful rhythm and immediacy in certain kinds of writing, such as that found in the Bible.

 Reading activity

Look at the following passage from 'The Pearl' by John Steinbeck. How would it read without the use of so many 'and's?

> And then Kino laid the rifle down, and he dug among his clothes, and then he held the great pearl in his hand. He looked into its surface and it was grey and ulcerous. Evil faces peered from it into his eyes, and he saw the light of burning.

Look up

Conjunction, Main clause, Subject.

Compound word

A compound word is made up of two or more words or word elements to form a new meaning. Compound words are generally nouns, although compound adjectives and verbs also occur.

 laptop, lighthouse, starfish, cashpoint

A Starfish

How compounds are formed

The process, sometimes called agglutination, whereby words are combined to form new 'compound' words is very common in German, where long strings of word parts are possible, but in English the number of elements is usually restricted to two or three.

> green + house → greenhouse
> life + boat → lifeboat
> cross + word → crossword
> ware + house + man → warehouseman

Sometimes the same two words can be combined in a different order to create two different new meanings.

> house + boat → boathouse/houseboat
> book + case → bookcase/casebook

The sum is more than the parts

Compounds provide a new meaning that is not present if the original words are separate.

> a lighthouse = a building with a signal light on top
> a light house = a well-lit house
> a Catseye = a glass reflector in the road
> a cat's eye = an eye of a cat

Hyphens in compounds

Some compound words are hyphenated, while others are written as one word. Some words are spelt both ways, particularly when they are new or unfamiliar.

> headbanger/head-banger
> crossbred/cross-bred

 **Writing activity**

Make a chart of compound words and see if you can spot any patterns. Think about whether the elements are nouns, verbs, adjectives etc. Do compounds lose their hyphens over time?

 **Look up**

Noun, Word origins.

Concord

Concord is another term used for agreement.

 Look up

Agreement.

Concrete noun

Concrete nouns are common nouns that refer to things that you can see, hear, taste, feel or smell. They therefore contrast with abstract nouns, although this distinction is one of meaning rather than of grammar.

Countable and uncountable

Concrete nouns can be either countable or uncountable.

 rice, money, flour   (*uncountable*)
table, cabbage, noise   (*countable*)

> **Using concrete nouns**
>
> In writing, concrete nouns can often be used to create vivid and exact impressions. Concrete nouns have often been used effectively in poetry.
>
> 📖 **Reading activity**
>
> Read 'Follower' by Seamus Heaney. How many concrete nouns does the poet use? What effect do they have?

 Look up

Abstract noun, Countable noun, Noun, Uncountable noun.

Conjugation

A conjugation is a way of listing the parts of a verb that go with particular pronouns.

How conjugations work

The order in which the various forms of the verb are listed with their pronouns is always the same.

	Singular	**Plural**
First person	I run	We run
Second person	You run	You run
Third person	He/She/It runs	They run

'We run' is therefore a clause made up of first person plural pronoun and verb. 'She runs' is a clause made up of a third person singular pronoun and verb. A verb preceded by 'you' is in the second person, but it is impossible to tell whether it is singular or plural without further information. (See box.)

Person, Pronoun, Verb.

Why 'you' is used as both a singular and a plural pronoun

'Thou' was once used as the singular pronoun, as in 'thou art'. 'Thou', 'thee', 'thy', 'thine' and 'thyself' were used when only one person was being referred to.

It was the custom to use 'thou' with people of a lower status. Lords would use it with servants, parents would use it with children. The exception to this was when people addressed God – presumably because they believed there was only one God, so he had to be addressed with the singular pronoun.

In order to avoid causing offence, 'you' gradually replaced 'thou' in all cases, although 'thou', 'thee', 'thy', 'thine' and 'thyself' are still found in prayers, older literary texts and in some dialects.

Conjunct

Conjuncts are words or phrases that help to make the connection between parts of a sentence clearer.

 to begin with, next, finally, to sum up, therefore, in that case

Using conjuncts

Conjuncts are used for various purposes:

- listing
   firstly, secondly, finally
- reinforcement
   moreover, above all
- result
   therefore, so
- concession
   nevertheless

Conjunction

A conjunction is a word that joins parts of sentences.

 and, but, if, although, as, where

Conjunctions at the beginning of sentences

Many traditional grammars warn that you should not start a sentence with a conjunction. But it is possible to do this to make a point more clearly or for emphasis (as in this sentence).

 Because you're late, we'll have to start again.

 Look up

Coordinating conjunction, Subordinating conjunction.

Connotation

Connotations are the ideas we have about a word in addition to its basic meaning (or 'denotation').

How's your motor?

jalopy, banger, car, wheels, limo

All of the above words denote an automobile, but 'jalopy' and 'banger' have negative connotations, 'car' has a neutral connotation and 'wheels' and 'limo' have positive connotations.

Different connotations

Connotations can often be highly personal. For some people the connotations of the word 'dog' might be 'loveable and faithful', whereas for others it might be 'fierce and contemptible'.

Using connotations

Writers frequently make use of a word's connotations to create effects. For instance, these lines occur in 'The Love Song of J. Alfred Prufrock', by T. S. Eliot:

> In the room the women come and go
> Talking of Michelangelo.

The connotations of the word 'Michelangelo' are to do with great art, and this suggests that the women are serious and interested in the arts, rather than, say, gossip.

 Look up

Denotation.

Coordinating conjunction

Coordinating conjunctions are conjunctions that join words, phrases or clauses together. The main coordinating conjunctions are 'and', 'but' and 'or'.

bat and ball	(*joining words*)
eight cups and four spoons	(*joining phrases*)
The house was old but the furniture was new.	(*joining clauses*)

Coordinating and subordinating conjunctions

Coordinating conjunctions imply that the things joined have an equal value, as opposed to subordinating conjunctions in which one clause is more important than the other.

False or pseudo coordination

False or pseudo-coordination occurs when a coordinating conjunction such as 'and' is used, but one of the joined elements is in fact more important than the other. In the following sentences, 'see' and 'asked' are the important elements.

 Try and see.
He went and asked.

Look up

Subordinating conjunction.

Copula verb

Copula verbs are linking verbs.

 be, seem, appear, become, remain, feel

Copula verbs in action

The most frequently used copula verb is 'be' when it links a subject with a complement.

 Gerum *is* a lawyer.

In the following example, 'grow' is a copula verb.

 Andrew grew more and more fearful.

(Verbs like 'feel' and 'grow' can also have objects, such as 'Andrew grew an apple tree from a seed.' In such cases they are not acting as copula verbs.)

Look up

Be, Complement, Subject.

Countable noun

Most types of nouns can divided into countable or uncountable categories. You can use 'a', 'an', 'the', 'some' and, of course, numbers with countable nouns.

 friend, car, holiday

Singular and plural
Most countable nouns have a singular and a plural form, although there are some exceptions, such as 'sheep'.

'Less' and 'fewer'
In very formal English 'fewer' is used before plural countable nouns and 'less' is used before uncountable nouns.

 There are fewer trees than there used to be.
There is also less grass.

Fewer trees

The frequently seen sign in supermarkets, 'Eight items or less', should therefore strictly read 'Eight items or fewer'.

 Look up
Formal language, Uncountable noun.

Dangling participle

See Hanging modifier.

Dash

The dash is a punctuation mark which looks like this —. In form it is a slightly longer version of the hyphen.

Use of the dash

The dash is a general purpose punctuation mark which is used in the place of commas, semi-colons and brackets. In sentences it represents a short pause. It is frequently used in informal writing.

> I left my coat – the new one – on the train.
> Sara made a new appointment at the dentist's – she had missed the last one.
> Don't forget to include an e-mail address – if you have one – and a day-time telephone number.

Dashes as inverted commas

In some books dashes are used as substitutes for inverted commas. The following example is from *Ulysses* by James Joyce.

– Well, sir, he began …
– I foresee, Mr Deasy said, that you will not remain here very long at this work. You were not born to be a teacher, I think. Perhaps I am wrong.
– A learner rather, Stephen said.

 Look up

Hyphen, Informal language, Inverted comma, Punctuation.

Defining relative clause

See Relative clause.

Definite article

See The.

Demonstrative pronoun

Demonstrative pronouns are pronouns that indicate where something is in relation to the speaker and listener (or, less commonly, to the writer and reader). They are:

this, that, those, these.

Using demonstrative pronouns

Demonstrative pronouns are used frequently in spoken English when it is clear from the context which particular object is being referred to. For instance, 'Give me that' would make perfect sense in a conversation if the speaker were pointing at something.

 Look up

Pronoun.

Denotation

The denotation of a word is the actual object or idea that it refers to. This is sometimes called the word's literal meaning or its 'dictionary' meaning.

 Look up

Connotation.

Descriptive grammar

Descriptive grammar looks at how language is used in everyday life. Descriptive grammarians base their rules on observations and do not make comments on how language ought to be used.

Look up

Grammar, Prescriptive grammar.

Dialect

A dialect is a language variety which differs from others in both vocabulary and grammar.

English dialects

There are many dialects of British English based on region and social class, as well as dialects such as American English, Indian English and Australian English.

> **Eg.** Get off of that chair.
> We was robbed.
> Hi, you all!
> He's late, innit?

Standard English is, grammatically speaking, a dialect.

Dialect and accent

Dialect is different from accent, which describes how words are pronounced.

 Speaking and listening activity

Very few people speak Standard English all the time. What are the grammatical characteristics of the dialect spoken in your area?

Look up

Accent, Standard English.

Dictionary

A dictionary is an alphabetical list of words with their meanings and other information. For anybody interested in grammar and words a dictionary is a key research tool, as the example on pp. 40–41 shows.

Headword: the word you want to find out about.

The definition of the word.

Related or alternative term.

Pronunciation: note the use of a phonetic alphabet. The dictionary will have a guide to this.

This shows that a word has a particular usage in a one variety of English.

Some words have special labels to show that they apply to a specialist area.

Etymology: the world's history.

Grammatical information.

Part of speech. Note that this word is listed with more than one.

Sense numbers: showing different meanings.

Example sentence or phrase.

Usage label.

Idiomatic phrase. If the phrase is well known it may appear as a headword.

Words formed by adding prefixes or suffixes to the headword. If the meaning is obvious no definition is given.

morse (mɔːs) *n.*

a clasp or fastening on a cope.

[C15: from Old French *mors,* from Latin *morsus* clasp, bite, from *mordēre* to bite]

Morse (mɔːs) *n.*

Samuel Finley Breese ('fɪnlɪ briːz). 1791-1872, U.S. inventor and painter. He invented the first electric telegraph and the Morse code.

Morse code *n.*

a telegraph code used internationally for transmitting messages. Letters, numbers, etc., are represented by groups of shorter dots and longer dashes, or by groups of the corresponding sounds, *dits* and *dahs,* the groups being separated by spaces.

Also called: **international Morse code.**

[C19: named after Samuel MORSE]

morsel ('mɔːsəl) *n.*

1. a small slice or mouthful of food.

2. a small piece; bit.

3. *Irish informal.* a term of endearment for a child.

[C13: from Old French, from *mors* a bite, from Latin *morsus,* from *mordēre* to bite]

Morse taper *n.*

Trademark, engineering. a taper that is one of a standard series used in the shank of tools to fit a matching taper in the mandrel of a machine tool.

[probably named after the *Morse* Twist Drill Co., Massachusetts, U.S.]

mort 1 (mɔːt) *n.*

a call blown on a hunting horn to signify the death of the animal hunted.

[C16: via Old French from Latin *mors* death]

mort 2 (mɔːt) *n.*

a great deal; a great many.

[possibly a shortened form of MORTAL used as an intensifier]

mortal ('mɔːtəl) *adj.*

1. (of living beings, esp. human beings) subject to death.

2. of or involving life or the world.

3. ending in or causing death; fatal: *a mortal blow.*

4. deadly or unrelenting: *a mortal enemy.*

5. of or like the fear of death; dire: *mortal terror.*

6. great or very intense: *mortal pain.*

7. possible: *there was no mortal reason to go.*

8. *Slang.* long and tedious: *for three mortal hours.*

— *n.*

9. a mortal being.

10. *Informal.* a person: *a mean mortal.*

[C14: from Latin *mortālis,* from *mors* death]

—**mortally** *adv.*

An extract from *Collins English Dictionary* (Electronic Version)

Directive

Directives are special sentences or clauses that give instructions. Directives are also known as imperatives or commands.

Directives in use
Directives use the verb in its base form and may use 'do' or 'let's'.

 Sit down!
Get away!
Let's go!
Do be quiet!

Conversations that use only directives sound very abrupt and even rude, so most of the time they are 'softened' by the use of polite phrases such as 'please', 'do you mind', 'could you' and so on.

 Look up

Base form, Clause, Special sentence.

Direct object

The direct object of a sentence is the thing acted on by a verb.

 I bought *a magazine*.

The direct object is often simply called the object of a sentence.

Direct and indirect objects
The direct object is in contrast to an indirect object.

 I bought her a magazine.

In the above sentence 'a magazine' is the direct object, and 'her' is the indirect object.

 Look up

Indirect object, Object.

Direct speech

Direct speech is a way of writing down speech which uses the actual words spoken.

Conventions used in direct speech

A number of conventions are used when direct speech is used in a story.

- The words spoken are usually placed inside quotation marks (also called inverted commas).

  Eg. 'Are you ready yet?'

- Labels such as 'she said' tell you who is speaking.

  Eg. 'Are you ready yet?' asked Mum.

- Speeches by different speakers are placed on separate lines.

  Eg. 'Are you ready yet?' asked Mum.
  'Yes,' replied Anna.

- The labels used to identify who is speaking are part of the same sentence as the speech, so that a comma, rather than a full stop, is used before the label.

  Eg. 'Yes,' replied Anna.

Direct speech is not a transcript

Direct speech is a conventional way of writing down speech. It does not usually attempt to capture all the features of real speech such as hesitations, sentences with false starts, irrelevant comments and asides, filler phrases and so on.

Using direct speech

In literature, direct speech, or dialogue, is a way in which readers can get to know characters at first hand rather than having to rely on statements made by the author. An excellent example of this is the opening chapter of *Pride and Prejudice* by Jane Austen, which consists almost entirely of dialogue.

 Look up

Indirect speech, Inverted comma, Transcript.

Disjunct

Disjuncts are words or phrases that report a speaker or writer's attitude.

Eg. frankly, honestly, fortunately, annoyingly, of course, to my surprise

When disjuncts are used

Disjuncts are not essential for grammatical completeness but they help to convey the speaker or writer's feelings. They would not be appropriate in, say, an encyclopaedia or a newspaper editorial as they help to make a writer's style 'chatty' or informal.

 Look up

Informal language.

Do

'Do' is an auxiliary verb that works with other verbs for a number of purposes.

The uses of 'do'

- 'Do' helps to form questions.

   Do you know where the teacher is?
   Why did Liam eat all the biscuits?

- 'Do' makes positive statements and directives more forceful.

   I do like ice cream!
   Do be quiet!

- 'Do' helps to form negative statements. In these cases it is usually shortened to 'doesn't' or 'don't'.

   Carol does not listen very carefully.
   Don't mind me!

- 'Do' can be used to invert (swap round) elements of a sentence for emphasis.

   Little did he realise that ...
   Only rarely does he come in before ten o'clock.

- 'Do' can be used to replace a verb or verb phrase used earlier in a sentence in order to avoid repetition.

   He likes you as much as I do.

- 'Do' is also found in old-fashioned poems where it has no meaning but helps the line to have the right number of syllables.

   did go *instead of* went
   did say *instead of* said

- 'Do' also has a very general sense of performing an action – verbs are often described as 'doing words'.

 Look up

Auxiliary verb, Directive.

Double negative

A double negative is the use of two negative terms in the same sentence.

> You don't know nothing.
> It is not unknown for explorers to get lost.

The 'incorrect' use of double negatives

In formal Standard English the use of double negatives such as those in the first two examples above is regarded as a fault, because logically the two negative terms cancel each other out (if you don't know nothing then you must know something). However, double negatives are quite common in speech, especially in certain dialects. They sound more emphatic than a single negative.

The 'correct' use of double negatives

Double negatives of the type 'not un-' are not condemned as a fault in formal Standard English, because the two negative elements cancel each other out to form a positive. In fact they are not uncommon, and are used to soften the force of an adjective. For instance, 'not unusual' is less emphatic than 'usual'.

 Look up

Dialect, Formal language, Standard English.

Emoticon

See Smiley.

English

English is the official language of over 280 million people in Britain, the United States, most parts of the Commonwealth and some other countries.

Old English

English arrived in this country with the Anglo-Saxons about 1500 years ago. In Old English the opening to the Lord's Prayer, 'Our Father who art in heaven, hallowed be thy name', looks like this:

Fæder ure
þu þe eart on heofunum
si þin nama gehalgod.

(The 'þ' symbol, which is called 'thorn', is pronounced 'th'.)

Old English had a system of 'weak' and 'strong' verbs. Weak verbs all had a regular past tense, but strong verbs varied, as in the examples below.

Modern verb	Base form	Past singular	Past plural	Past participle
bite	bitan	bat	biton	biten
creep	creopan	creap	crupon	cropen
drink	drincan	dranc	druncon	druncen
steal	stelan	stæl	stælon	stolen

In Old English words were inflected, that is, they had different forms according to what work they were doing in a sentence. Anglo-Saxon students had to learn not just one word for 'stone' but separate words for 'of the stone', 'to the stone' etc. They also had to remember if 'stone' was masculine, feminine or neuter.

Singular	Stone (masculine)	Word (neuter)	Gift (feminine)
Nominative (= subject)	stan	word	giefu
Genitive ('of the …' etc.)	stanes	wordes	giefe
Dative ('to the …' etc.)	stane	worde	giefe
Accusative (= object)	stan	word	giefe
Plural			
Nominative	stanas	word	giefa
Genitive	stana	worda	giefa
Dative	stanum	wordum	giefum
Accusative	stanas	word	giefa

The inflection of nouns meant that their form rather than their order showed whether they were the subject or object of a sentence. As a result, word order was not very important. For instance, the two sentences below would have meant the same in Old English.

Seo cwen geseah þone guman.

þone guman geseah seo cwen. } The woman saw the man.

'The man saw the woman' would have been:

Se guma geseah þa cwen.

Changes to Old English

The Anglo-Saxon peoples, who had invaded and displaced the Celtic Britons, were invaded in their turn by the Vikings and the Normans. The Vikings raided at first, but in the northern and eastern parts of the country they settled in an area called the Danelaw. Today over 1400 'English' place names are of Viking origin, particularly those ending in '-by', '-thorpe' and '-thwaite'. The Vikings, who spoke a language now known as Old Norse, gave us many words.

 egg, garden, get, leg, skirt, skip, skin, sky

Modern English also owes the words 'they', 'their', 'them', 'both', 'same', 'till' and 'with' to Old Norse. These are unusual words for a language to borrow as they are 'grammatical' words. It has also been suggested that the use of Old Norse and Old English together over quite a long period of time was one of the reasons why the Old English inflection system disappeared.

The Normans spoke Old French and introduced the first English spelling problems. They may also have introduced the first social distinctions in the English language. Anglo-Saxon scribes wrote 'cw'; the Norman scribes introduced 'qu'. They also tended to use 'o' instead of 'u' in words like 'come', 'son' and 'love' (which even in Shakespeare's day rhymed with 'prove'). Words we use today for cooked food tend to be Old French, whereas the names of the living animals come from Old English. For example:

Old English origin	Old French origin
cow	beef
sheep	mutton
swine	pork
deer	venison

Middle English

After the Norman Conquest of 1066 Old French became the official language of England. It was used at Court, by administrators and by lawyers, but little effort was made to encourage ordinary people to learn it. Richard I (1189–99) probably spoke no English at all, but by 1381 Richard II was able to address rebellious peasants in English. In 1362 a law was passed which said that English should always be spoken in law courts as not many people spoke French. Most official and learned writing, however, was done in Latin.

The words that came into English from Old French at this time tended to involve the 'official' aspects of life, such as:

- government

  Eg. parliament, sovereign, royal, minister, nation

- religion

  Eg. creator, confession, saint, friar

- the law

  Eg. crime, constable, judge, justice

- the army

  Eg. lieutenant, sergeant, enemy, combat

Changes in Middle English

The numerous borrowings from French and Latin at this period seem to have established a habit that English has never lost. English speakers have never been afraid of introducing new and 'foreign' terms into the language.

The Middle English period saw the loss of many Old English words, such as 'lyft' for 'air', 'earm' for 'poor' and 'aetheling' for 'noble'. It also saw major changes in pronunciation and in spelling conventions.

By the time English had been re-established as the official language, at least five major dialects had developed so that one writer complained that 'some use strange wlaffing, chytering, harring and garring grisbitting' to express themselves. Spelling was even less standardised. Here are some of the ways 'might' was written in Middle English manuscripts:

mayht mahte mihhte micht miytest mithe myght.

There was no such thing as standard English or standard spelling at this time.

One of the most famous works in Middle English is Geoffrey Chaucer's *Canterbury Tales*. It begins:

> Whan Aprille with his shoures soote
> The droghte of March hath perced to the roote
> And bathed every veyne in swich licour
> Of which vertue engendred is the flour.

Or, in modern English:

> When April with his sweet showers
> Has pierced the drought of March to the root
> And bathed every vein in such liquid
> From which strength the flower is engendered.

The emergence of Modern English

London, the capital of the country, and the two main universities, Oxford and Cambridge, were in the East Midlands dialect area, and this dialect eventually gave rise to Modern English.

In 1476 William Caxton set up his first printing press in London. He had to choose the spellings he would use from his authors' manuscripts. Like most printers he decided to use a 'house style', a consistent set of spellings within his publishing house, rather than simply copying the words directly from the manuscripts.

It took around two hundred years for the idea of 'correct' spellings to develop, but by the time of the English Civil War (1641–8) printers and writers had agreed on more or less common sets of conventions. The Civil War period was when printers finally stopped adding letters to words to help them line up the right-hand edge of their texts.

The development of Modern English

The development of Modern English, from about 1500 onwards, coincided with the spread of English throughout the world through trade and conquest.

The number of words in English grew tremendously in the 16th century for four main reasons:

- Trade and exploration meant that English-speaking people came into contact with new ideas, new techniques, new peoples and new languages. New words were borrowed or invented freely.
- The 16th century was the period of the rediscovery of Latin and Greek learning. Scholars consciously mined the old learning for new, striking or more exact terms.
- The final decline of the inflection system meant that many words were used in new ways. For instance, nouns were used as verbs.
- The older practices of creating new words either by adding suffixes and prefixes or by making new compounds continued, but with fresh energy.

One result of so much energy and enthusiasm about words is that English has one of the largest vocabularies of any world language.

Many words came into English in the 16th or 17th century.

> 'balcony', 'coffee', 'volcano' (Italian)
> 'banana', 'guitar' (Spanish)
> 'cruise', 'landscape', 'yacht' (Dutch)
> 'curry' (Tamil)
> 'democracy' (Greek via French)
> 'education', 'invite', 'muscle' (Latin)
> 'guru' (Hindi)
> 'ketchup' (Chinese)

In the 18th century attempts were made to get English under control. Grammar books and style books were produced in great numbers, and the first great dictionary of the English language was published by Dr Johnson in 1755.

Many of the decisions made at this time are still with us today. For instance, the poet John Dryden was one of the first people to popularise the idea that you shouldn't end sentences with prepositions. Dr Johnson thought that if possible words should show where they had come from. He knew that 'debt' came originally from the Latin 'debitus', and so gave the word a 'b' which it had never had before and which no one has ever pronounced.

English today

Modern English grammar has changed little since the end of the 18th century. Grammarians have succeeded in driving double negatives out of polite conversation. The spread of education has meant that more people have access to Standard English, and there has been a corresponding decline in the use of regional dialects.

Most changes have taken place in vocabulary, where science and technology have introduced many new words and improved communications have given people who can speak English access to the entire world.

World English

Modern English has spread all over the world, and as it has spread it has changed. It is no longer strictly accurate to speak of 'English'. This book really only deals with British English; there are different sets of rules for American English, Australian English, Indian English, Jamaican English, South African English and so on.

Look up

Grammar, Inflection, Standard English, Word origins.

Etymology

Etymology is the study of where words came from and how their meanings change over time.

Etymology and usage

The etymology of a word does not affect how it is used in present-day English, although sometimes people try to restrict how a word is used by reference to its etymology. For instance, it has been stated that 'a lot' should not be used to mean 'many' because 'a lot' originally meant simply a portion or share.

Likewise, although 'decimate' is now used to mean simply 'destroy', as in 'France decimated Brazil in the final', it originally meant 'destroy a tenth of' (from Latin *decem* – as the Romans killed every tenth man of a mutinous army). Some people therefore still use it only to mean 'destroy a large proportion of', as in 'The Black Death decimated the population of Europe.'

 Look up

Morphology, Word origins.

Exclamation

An exclamation is a type of sentence expressing strong feelings.

Exclamations as special sentences

Many exclamations are 'minor' or 'special' sentences as they lack a normal sentence structure.

 How true! Brilliant! You don't say! Alas! Oh! Really!

Using exclamations

Exclamations are much commoner in speech than in writing, as they are often used by listeners to make short statements that show they are paying attention. In writing, exclamations, or sentences ending in exclamation marks, are characteristic of an informal style. For instance, the sentence 'We had left our coats on the bus', without an exclamation mark, is simply a statement. With an exclamation mark it shows more about how the writer felt about the event.

 Look up

Exclamation mark, Informal language, Question, Smiley, Special sentence.

Exclamation mark

The exclamation mark is a punctuation mark which looks like this **!** .

How exclamation marks are used

An exclamation mark is used to show the way a sentence should be pronounced. They must be used in imperative or directive sentences.

  Stop!
Be quiet!
Look out!

Changing the tone

When an exclamation mark is added to a statement it changes the tone of the statement.

  It was cold. → It was cold! (*stronger tone*)
They were very silly. → They were very silly! (*less serious tone*)

I am going to my room. → I am going to my room! (*angry tone*)

 Look up

Directive, Punctuation.

False subject

False subjects are used to emphasise part of a sentence or clause.

 There was a sudden noise.
There is no money for treats.

'There' in such sentences has very little meaning on its own. It is sometimes known as 'existential there', as it simply means 'that situation described in the sentence exists'.

Finite verb

Finite refers to any form of the verb that is inflected for grammatical features such as person, number (singular and plural) and tense.

Finite and non-finite
Finite verbs take subjects and can form sentences on their own. The non-finite forms of verbs, which consist of infinitives, participles or verb groups beginning with a participle, cannot form sentences on their own.

 He thinks, Think about it, She thought   (*finite*)
To think, Thinking about it, Having thought
about it   (*non-finite*)

Look up
Inflection, Non-finite verb, Person, Tense.

Formal language

Formal language is speech or writing that uses the strictest rules and pays the most careful attention to such things as Standard English.

Features of formal language

Formal language does not have its own special grammar, but it might be expected to:

- use more complex sentences than informal language
- contain more sentences in the passive
- avoid contractions such as 'can't'
- make full use of specialist terms
- avoid colloquialisms and slang
- avoid constructions that have been criticised by grammarians, such as hanging modifiers, split infinitives and double negatives.

Using formal language

Formal language is used most often in serious situations, for instance in a speech in court or in a scientific report. When it is used properly its purpose is to make meaning as clear as possible. Formal language can also be found in news reports on television and radio, speeches in debates, legal documents, encyclopaedia entries, application forms and so on.

 Look up

Colloquial language, Complex sentence, Double negative, Hanging modifier, Informal language, Passive voice, Slang, Split infinitive, Standard English.

Fronting

Fronting is the movement of part of a sentence to the beginning to make that part stand out.

Fronting in action

Many sentences begin with their subject.

 Martina went to the gym on Saturday.

However, if the speaker or writer wishes to focus attention on *when* Martina went to the gym, the sentence can be rewritten:

On Saturday Martina went to the gym.

A focus on *where* Martina went on Saturday might produce the slightly odd sentence:

To the gym Martina went on Saturday.

Look up
Inversion.

Full stop

A full stop is a punctuation mark which indicates the end of the sentence. It tells the reader to pause briefly in his or her reading.

Full stops are important
Full stops cannot be omitted unless they are replaced by either a question mark or an exclamation mark.

 The storm was gathering on the horizon.
Harriet arrived.

Full stops in abbreviations
Full stops are also used with some abbreviations.

 e.g., a.m., i.e.

Using full stops
A knowledge of how sentences work is essential for the correct use of full stops.

✐ Writing activity
Add full stops to the following paragraph.

Stephanie was walking home when she heard a loud noise it came from her street she ran quickly towards the corner as did several others when she arrived she saw that two cars had collided

Look up
Punctuation.

Future tense

The future tense is the tense of the verb used when the writer or speaker wants to refer to an event occurring after the time of writing or speaking.

Forming the future

It is often said that the future tense is formed by using either 'shall' or 'will' with the base form of a verb.

 You will leave, I shall go.

In fact there are several ways of talking about the future in English:

- using 'going to':

     I am going to get my exam results tomorrow.

I am going to get my exam results tomorrow

- using part of the verb 'be' plus an '-ing' form:

     I am seeing the doctor on Tuesday.

(Note: this form of the present tense usually has a time indicator.)

- using the simple present tense:

     I play football next week.

Shall and will

Old fashioned grammars stated that 'shall' should be used with the first person and 'will' with the second and third persons. Nowadays, however, 'will' tends to be used in most statements and 'shall' is more common in questions.

 Shall I go?

Look up

Base form, Tense.

Gender

Gender is a way of categorising nouns by the sex of the thing referred to (that is, masculine, feminine or neuter).

Gender in English
English, unlike French or German, does not have grammatical gender, but some words differ according to whether they refer to women or men.

 waiter/waitress, comedian/comedienne, nurse/male nurse

Gender and sexism
Nowadays it regarded as sexist to make distinctions based on gender, and many of the feminine forms of words are dropping out of use. Similarly, it is no longer considered correct to use words that are specifically male, such as fireman or chairman. (Firefighter and chair or chairperson are used instead.)

Gender and pronouns
Problems occur with the use of pronouns, as English does not have a gender-neutral term for referring to people. 'It' can be used of things, but many people feel uncomfortable constantly using 'he or she', 'him or her', 's/he', 'he/she' etc. Sometimes 'they' is used when both men and women are being referred to, but this causes problems with agreement as 'they' is a plural pronoun.

Look up
Agreement, Pronoun.

Grammar

Grammar is the rules of a language, which describe how words can be combined to form phrases, clauses and sentences.

The early history of grammar: Jonson & Johnson

In medieval Europe the only grammar that was seriously studied was that of Latin, but after the Renaissance people began to look more closely at the rules of their own languages. English grammar has developed with the language, but until the 17th century little was done to lay down rules about the way people spoke and wrote. This was a period of great growth and change in English, when such writers as Ben Jonson, Francis Bacon and William Shakespeare were inventing new words and giving new meanings to old ones. So much change caused worry and anxiety and people began to look for guidance.

At this time there were no agreed spellings and it was therefore impossible to make a spelling mistake! However, a dictionary of 'hard words' was published by Robert Cawdrey in 1604; this was followed by many others, culminating in Dr Johnson's great *Dictionary of the English Language* in 1755.

As dictionaries grew, so too did interest in grammar. Two early grammars were written by Ben Jonson, published in 1640, and John Wallis, published in 1653. Jonson believed that 'custom with the consent of the learned' was the best guide to correct usage, but Wallis complained that Jonson had 'forced English too rigidly into the mould of Latin'. This debate about the difference between how people ought to speak and how they actually speak has been at the centre of ideas about grammar ever since.

Grammar in the 18th century

In the 18th century many writers complained of the 'decay' of English, and grammars began to appear in response. One of the most successful was Murray's *English Grammar* (1794). This was a prescriptive grammar, describing how English ought to be spoken and written, which remained popular in schools for the next hundred years (popular with teachers, that is).

Several of the 'rules' of grammar that are still argued about today emerged during the 18th century. For instance, the ideas that you should not split infinitives or end sentences with prepositions came from writers who had studied Latin grammar.

Descriptive and prescriptive grammar

Modern grammar is still either descriptive or prescriptive. Prescriptive grammar is needed by foreign language speakers who wish to learn English. They need a set of rules on how Standard

English is usually spoken and written. These rules are based on observations of real English, however, rather than on the preconceived ideas of certain grammarians. Descriptive grammar looks at how speakers and writers of English actually use English, and derives its rules from such observations. Grammars of this type might deal with Standard British English, Australian English, Indian English or any one of the many dialects of English. These kinds of books are often called reference grammars.

Specialist areas

The study of grammar today is divided into several major areas. These include the study of syntax (how words combine to create meaning), morphology (how words change over time), semantics (the relationships between words and their meanings), sociolinguistics (the effect of social context on language), stylistics (the way people choose particular types of language) and phonology (the sound system of language).

Computers and grammar

The study of all areas of grammar has been greatly helped by the use of computers and the development of language databases (or 'corpora') such as COBUILD. Instead of relying on the observations of individuals or small groups, computer databases allow accurate statistical analysis, and because they record spoken language as well as written, they allow greater focus on spoken English than in the past.

Look up

Descriptive grammar, Dialect, English, Linguistics, Morphology, Prescriptive grammar, Standard English.

Hanging modifier

Hanging modifiers are verbal phrases such as participles and infinitives which do not clearly and logically refer to a noun or pronoun in the sentences in which they occur. ('Hanging participles' and 'dangling participles' are other terms used.)

Hanging modifiers in action

In each of the sentences below the sense intended by the writer is clear, but as the modifying phrase is not connected logically it is said to be hanging or dangling.

 To improve at football, practice is necessary. (*infinitive*)
When two months old, her mother walked to London. (*subordinate clause*)
Rushing to meet the deadline, mistakes occurred. (*participle*)
Sleeping in mine garden, a serpent stung me. (*participle*)

In the last example, which occurs in *Hamlet*, Shakespeare clearly intended us to understand that it was the speaker who was asleep, not the serpent, but logically it appears as if the serpent was sleeping.

 Writing activity

Rewrite the four example sentences above so that they are more logical.

Look up

Infinitive, Participle.

Have

Apart from being a main verb in itself (meaning 'possess' or 'hold', amongst other things), 'have' is an auxiliary verb which helps to form the perfect tense of other verbs.

How 'have' works as an auxiliary

- 'Have' in the present tense + a past participle gives the present perfect tense.

  Eg. I have waited.

- 'Have' in the present tense + 'been' + a present participle forms the continuous present perfect tense.

  Eg. She has been listening.

- 'Have' in the past tense + a past participle forms the past perfect tense.

  Eg. We had already talked about it.

- 'Have' in the past tense + 'been' + a present participle forms the continuous past perfect tense.

  Eg. They had been waiting for hours.

- 'Will' or 'shall' + 'have' + a past participle gives the future perfect tense.

  Eg. He will have finished by now.

- 'Will' or 'shall' + 'have' + 'been' + a present participle forms the continuous future perfect tense.

  Eg. By the time you get there, you will have been walking for ages.

Look up

Auxiliary verb.

Hypercorrection

Hypercorrection is a mistake in grammar made when trying too hard to follow the rules of Standard English.

Not sure of the rules

Hypercorrection often occurs when people are aware of a grammatical rule but are not quite sure of how it works. For instance, many people know that you should always say 'my friend and I' in a sentence like

My friend and I went to the cinema

instead of

Me and my friend went to the cinema.

Ships in the Night: A Cautionary Tale
by Lawrence Bush

I had only just arrived at the club when I bumped into Roger. After we had exchanged a few pleasantries, he lowered his voice and asked, 'What do you think of Martha and I as a potential twosome?'

'That,' I replied, 'would be a mistake. Martha and me is more like it.'

'You're interested in Martha?'

'I'm interested in clear communication.'

'Fair enough,' he agreed. 'May the best man win.' Then he sighed. 'Here I thought we had a clear path to becoming a very unique couple.'

'You couldn't be a very unique couple, Roger.'

'Oh? And why is that?'

'Martha couldn't be a little pregnant, could she?'

'Say what? You think that Martha and me ...'

'Martha and I.'

'Oh.' Roger blushed and set down his drink. 'Gee, I didn't know.'

'Of course you didn't,' I assured him. 'Most people don't.'

'I feel very badly about this.'

'You shouldn't say that: I feel bad ...'

'Please, don't,' Roger said. 'If anyone's at fault here, it's me!'

Based on a Laugh of the Day, January 1997

Sometimes, as the above story shows, concentrating on 'correct' grammar does not improve communication.

Hypercorrection occurs when, remembering this, people say

He gave it to my friend and I.

instead of

He gave it to my friend and me.

When hypercorrection hoccurs
Hypercorrection most commonly happens when people are 'on their best behaviour'. It can also be seen when people add an 'h' to words that don't need them, because they have been told not to drop their 'h's.

 I ham honoured to meet Your Majesty.

⌐Look up

Standard English.

Hyphen

The hyphen is a punctuation mark which looks like this - . In form it is a slightly shorter version of the dash.

Use of the hyphen
Hyphens are used to join the parts of compound words.

 user-friendly, over-used, light-headed, soft-headed

They are also used to join the syllables of words that are broken at the end of a line of writing.

Hyphens in adjectival phrases
Hyphens can also be used to give phrases, clauses or sentences an adjectival function.

 He gave me an oh-no-you-don't look.

Dropped hyphens
When a word combination has been in use for a long time the hyphen is frequently dropped.

 Software
Lighthouse

⌐Look up

Compound word, Dash, Punctuation.

Imperative

See Directive.

Indefinite article

See A, an.

Indefinite comparison

An indefinite comparison is a comparison that does not make it clear which two things are being compared.

 Anne looks better.
Brian's Batteries Last Longer

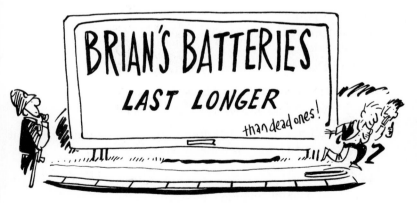

How indefinite comparisons are used

Indefinite comparisons leave the questions 'better than what?', 'longer than what?' etc. unanswered. They are very popular in advertising, as they can be used to create a generally good impression, without making specific claims that can be tested.

 **Look up**

Comparative.

Indefinite pronoun

Indefinite pronouns are pronouns that take the place of a person, place, thing or quality that is not specified.

 one, anybody, everyone, everything, something, either, both, much

Indefinite pronouns and agreement

Indefinite pronouns can sometimes cause problems with agreement. For instance, the 'every' part of the word 'everybody' seems to refer to several things, but everybody is a singular pronoun.

 Everybody *is* excited.

Therefore the sentence 'Everybody should get their books' should read 'Everybody should get his or her books'. However, sometimes 'their' is used deliberately to avoid the phrase 'his or her', which some people consider clumsy.

'One' or 'you'?

Another problem is caused by 'one'. This is sometimes used in formal sentences.

 One should always try to avoid conflict.

In less formal sentences 'you' is used.

 You should always try to avoid conflict.

One should not use the two forms in the same sentence, as it makes you sound uncertain about one's tone!

Look up

Agreement, Formal language, Pronoun.

Indirect object

The indirect object 'receives' the object of a sentence.

 Salma bought *her mother* a birthday card.

In this sentence 'a birthday card' is the object of the sentence, which is 'received' by her mother. 'Her mother' is therefore the indirect object.

Different kinds of indirect object
The indirect object can be:

● a pronoun:

Eg. Kevin drove the car for *us*.

● a noun phrase:

Eg. I sent *all my friends* invitations.

● or a noun:

Eg. I lent *Maria* the book.

'To' and 'for'
Sentences with indirect objects have two forms:

Eg. I lent *Maria* the book *or* I lent the book *to Maria*.
I wrote *the milkman* a note *or* I wrote a note *for the milkman*.

In the second form, the indirect object is always introduced by the preposition 'to' or 'for'.

Look up
Direct object, Object, Pronoun.

Indirect speech

See Reported speech.

Infinitive

The infinitive is the base form of a verb with 'to' in front of it.

 to work, to be, to talk

Base form, Split infinitive.

Inflection

Inflections are changes to a word for grammatical reasons. These changes affect nouns and verbs.

Inflections in nouns

Nouns are inflected:

- when 's' is added to show a plural form:

  hat → hats

- when an apostrophe is added to show possession:

  Martin → Martin's hat

Inflections in verbs

Verbs are inflected:

- in the third person singular form:

  eat → she eats

- in the present participle:

  look → looking

- in the past simple:

  play → she played

- in the past participle:

  write → written.

Inflections and word order

Because inflections show the grammatical function of a word, languages that use them do not need to depend on word order for their meaning. The meaning is clear from the inflected forms of the words. One of the most significant changes in English has been the loss of inflections since the Old English period. In English, therefore, word order is very important.

Look up

English, Morphology

Informal language

Informal language is friendly in tone and quite relaxed in structure.

Different kinds of informality

The meaning of 'informal' changes with the context of your speech or writing. For instance, an informal interview would be relaxed and chatty in tone but it would seem very serious compared to an informal conversation between friends. Similarly, an informal article in a newspaper, such as a gossip column, would be much more highly structured than an informal note.

Characteristics of informal language

Formal writing or speech is language on its best behaviour: no short cuts are taken and every effort is made to make sure that grammar, syntax and style are 'correct'. Informal language is more relaxed in tone. There are many levels of informal language, but in general it will:

- be personal rather than impersonal
- be addressed to a known or familiar audience
- use contractions such as 'it's' or 'can't'
- use more comment clauses
- use active rather than passive verbs
- address the reader as 'you'
- make use of colloquial language.

Look up

Colloquial language, Comment, Formal language, Slang.

Intensifier

Intensifiers are words or phrases that strengthen the meaning of other words or phrases. Intensifiers are adverbs or adjectives.

 It was *very* hot
Karla was *bitterly* disappointed.
I like him *a lot*.
The film was *utter* rubbish.

'So' and 'such'

In formal Standard English some people object to the use of 'so' as an intensifier.

 I was so cold.

They argue that 'so' should be followed by 'that' to form a sentence like, 'I was *so* cold *that* my teeth chattered.'

Similar objections are made to 'such' as it is used in a sentence like, 'It was such a hot day.'

Look up

Adjective, Adverb, Formal language, Standard English.

Interrogative mood

See Mood, Question.

Interrogative pronoun

Interrogative pronouns are pronouns used to ask questions. They are:

who, which, whom, whose, what
whoever, whichever, whatever

'Whose' and 'who's'

There is sometimes confusion between 'whose' and 'who's'. 'Whose' is used in the sense of belonging to, as in 'Whose jacket is this?' 'Who's' is a contraction of 'who is'.

Look up

Pronoun, Relative pronoun.

Intransitive verb

Intransitive verbs are verbs that do not take a direct object.

 arrive, come, fall, appear, die

Transitive and intransitive
Some verbs have both intransitive and transitive uses.

 Phoebe won.   (*intransitive*)
Phoebe won the prize.   (*transitive*)

 Look up
Direct object, Transitive verb.

Inversion

Inversion is swapping the order of the subject and the verb to make the action stand out.

 he said → said he
the sun came out → out came the sun

Inversion and fronting
Inversion is often used alongside fronting.

 To the circus went the family.

Reading activity

The unusual order of words produced by inversion is popular in children's rhymes.

   Pop! goes the weasel
   Down came the rain
   Said Simple Simon to the pieman

Look in a collection of children's rhymes for more examples. Why do you think inversion is so common in children's rhymes?

 **Look up**

Fronting.

Inverted comma

The inverted comma is a punctuation mark which looks like this '
or this " (open inverted commas) or this ' or this ". Inverted commas are also known as speech marks or quotation marks.

How inverted commas are used

Inverted commas are used to show the beginning and end of direct speech, titles or quotations.

   'Curiouser and curiouser,' said Alice.
   Martha asked, 'Which way now?'
   The words 'To be or not to be' begin one of the most
      famous speeches in 'Hamlet'.

 Look up

Direct speech.

Irregular

Irregular means not following any obvious pattern.

Irregular forms

Noun plurals, comparisons and some verb forms can be irregular.

- Irregular plurals:

  > Eg. child → children
  > sheep → sheep
  > mouse → mice
  > foot → feet

- Irregular comparisons:

  > Eg. good, better, best
  > bad, worse, worst
  > much (*or* many), more, most

- Irregular verb forms:

Eg. Simple present	Simple past	Past participle
I see	I saw	seen
I run	I ran	run
I put	I put	put
I speak	I spoke	spoken

Is English an irregular language?

People tend to remember or notice irregularities more than things that follow a pattern, and this sometimes creates a false impression that English is a very irregular language. There are fewer than 300 irregular verbs, for instance, but these verbs are amongst the most commonly used. Similarly, the majority of nouns form regular plurals, but again the exceptions are words that commonly occur.

Even spelling is not as irregular as many people think. About 84 per cent of English spellings conform to a general pattern, and only 3 per cent of words are spelled in very unpredictable ways.

Look up

Comparative, English, Plural, Regular.

Jargon

Jargon is a particular type of language spoken by a particular group of people.

Why jargon is used

Most areas of life have words or expressions that mean little to non-specialists. They are described as jargon when specialists introduce them into ordinary speech or writing to mystify others. Computer experts talk of 'ROM' and 'RAM' or 'bits' and 'bytes', whereas builders might talk of 'RSJs' or a 'screed'.

The use of jargon helps people in the same group or profession to identify each other and to exclude others. Sometimes groups make up a jargon deliberately to exclude others. An example of this is Cockney rhyming slang, which was originally a thieves' jargon.

Lexical verb

See Verb.

Linguistics

Linguistics is the study of language in its broadest sense. There are many branches of the subject, including:

- historical linguistics: the study of how languages change over time;
- contrastive linguistics: the study of two or more languages at a particular point in time;
- applied linguistics: this deals with the practical application of linguistic insights in such areas as grammar teaching or the teaching of foreign languages.

 Look up

Grammar.

Main clause

In a complex sentence, the main clause usually contains the main information of the whole sentence. A main clause makes sense on its own.

 Rhianon made some tea when she arrived home.

Complex sentence, Subordinate clause.

Metalanguage

A metalanguage is a language used to discuss language.

Grammar as a metalanguage

English grammar is the metalanguage used to discuss English. It has evolved over the years and many different naming systems have been developed. For instance, some grammars refer to the 'present participle' whilst other grammars prefer the label '-ing form'.

Grammar.

Middle English

See English.

Minor sentence

See Special sentence.

Modal auxiliary

See Modal verb.

Modal verb

Modal verbs (or modal auxiliaries) are verbs that modify (or add meaning to) other verbs. They are:

can, may, will, shall, must, ought, need, dare, could, might, would should

How modal verbs modify meaning
The chief use of modals is to modify the meaning of the verbs to which they are attached. This varies between possibility (can) and necessity (must).

 You can go   (*going is possible, or you have permission to go*)

You may go   (*going is suggested, or you have permission to go*)

You might go   (*going is a possibility*)

You should go   (*going is strongly suggested or obligatory*)

You must go   (*you have no choice about going*)

Aspects of modal verbs
Most modal verbs do not have 's' forms in the third person singular, nor do they have infinitives or participles. They generally make questions by inversion (e.g. 'I can' → 'Can I?') and they can be made negative by the addition of 'not' or '-n't' (e.g. cannot, can't).

Using modal verbs
Modal verbs are commonly used in forming questions and question tags.

Can I go to the cinema?
Judith must be here, mustn't she?

Modals are also used to give advice and make suggestions. They therefore frequently occur in speech or writing that tries to influence behaviour. For instance, the lottery slogan 'It could be you!' suggests the possibility of winning; it is stronger than 'It might be you!' and less definite than 'It will be you!'

A
B
C
D
E
F
G
H
I
J
K
L
M
N
O
P
Q
R
S
T
U
V
W
X
Y
Z

Look up

Inversion, Question, Question tag.

Mood

'Mood' is the term used to describe the kind of sentence a verb forms.

The moods described

The moods are: indicative, imperative, interrogative and subjunctive. These terms are now considered rather old fashioned, as they relate more closely to aspects of Latin grammar than they do to English.

- Some sentences are in the indicative mood, that is, they make a statement:

  Eg. The door is open.

- Some sentences are in the imperative mood:

  Eg. Open the door!

- Some sentences are in the interrogative mood:

  Eg. Is the door open?

- Some sentences are in the subjunctive mood:

  Eg. If I were you I would open the door.

Look up

Directive, Question, Subjunctive, Verb.

Morphology

Morphology is the study of the form and structure of words, including the way they are inflected, how they combine, how they change and their etymology.

Look up

English, Etymology, Grammar, Inflection, Word origins.

Netiquette

Netiquette is an informal system of rules and regulations for use in e-mail and on the Internet or World Wide Web.

The importance of netiquette

Netiquette primarily consists of rules of polite behaviour and is comparable to etiquette. Not keeping to these rules can cause misunderstanding or annoyance. Many of the rules relate to sharing a 'public' message space and the need to keep messages short because it costs money to be connected to the Internet.

Rules of netiquette

Some rules of Netiquette are:

- Do not write in capital letters. This is like shouting in speech and is considered impolite.
- Do not use the usual opening and closing conventions for letters in print (e.g. 'Dear James' or 'Yours sincerely').
- Use asterisks (*) before and after a word if you want to emphasise it.
- Be careful about using irony or sarcasm. Readers can't see facial expressions or hear tone of voice, and so statements intended as jokes can be taken seriously.
- Jokes can be shown by using a 'smiley' or 'emoticon' such as :-). But you should not use too many of these.
- Avoid 'flames'. A flame is an angry responses to a message. Exchanges of flames, or 'flame wars', can be very annoying to other readers on a list or newsgroup.
- Always include the subject of a message in the subject line.
- Messages should be relatively short and to the point.
- Do not forward other people's e-mail messages without the author's permission.
- Include the parts of the original message being responded to in new e-mails or 'posts' to newsgroups.

Net abbreviations

Net abbreviations are used to shorten messages, avoid repetitive phrases and to speed up typing.

	BTW	By the way
	FAQ	Frequently asked questions
	FWIW	For what it's worth
	FYI	For your information
	IAE	In any event
	IMO	In my opinion
	IMCO	In my considered opinion
	IOW	In other words
	NRN	No reply necessary
	OTOH	On the other hand
	ROFL	Rolling on floor laughing
	TIA	Thanks in advance (also AtDhVaAnNkCsE)
	TIC	Tongue in cheek

Look up

Smiley.

Non-defining relative clause

See Relative clause.

Non-finite verb

Non-finite refers to forms of verbs such as infinitives, participles and verb groups beginning with a participle which cannot form sentences on their own.

to know what happened
knowing what happened
having known what happened

Look up

Finite verb, Infinitive, Participle.

Noun

Nouns are words that name objects or qualities. They can be preceded by articles ('a', 'an', 'the' and 'some') and have singular and plural forms.

Types of noun
There are several different types of noun.

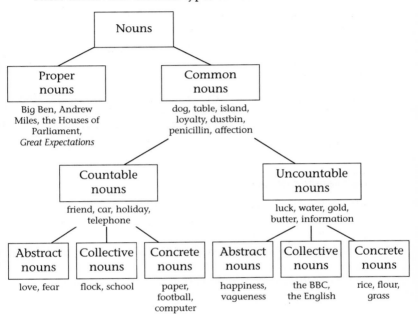

Singular and plural
Most nouns can be singular, referring to one thing, or plural, referring to more than one thing. The normal way of making a noun plural is by adding '-s' or '-es'.

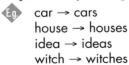   car → cars
house → houses
idea → ideas
witch → witches

Some nouns are always plural in form.

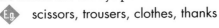   scissors, trousers, clothes, thanks

A few nouns have no plural form.

> **Eg** sheep, deer

Other nouns have irregular plurals.

> **Eg** child → children
> foot → feet
> mouse → mice
> stimulus → stimuli

Uncountable nouns do not have plural forms but can be referred to in plural instances by using another noun followed by 'of'.

> **Eg** strokes of luck, pats of butter, pieces of information

Using nouns

Nouns, along with verbs, form a basic part of language. They are amongst the first words we learn as children and feature in the vast majority of sentences, sometimes in the form of pronouns. Accurate and clear writing can often be achieved by the careful choice of nouns and verbs.

Reading activity

One of the great advantages of English is the richness of its vocabulary. This allows writers to choose words precisely and to create a wide range of effects.

In John Masefield's poem 'Cargoes', for instance, he does little more than list ships and cargoes, but his precise choice of nouns gives a very different atmosphere to each verse.

> Quinquireme of Nineveh from distant Ophir
> Rowing home to haven in sunny Palestine,
> With a cargo of ivory,
> And apes and peacocks,
> Sandalwood, cedarwood, and sweet white wine ...
>
> Dirty British coaster with a salt-caked smoke stack
> Butting through the Channel in the mad March days,
> With cargo of Tyne coal,
> Road-rail, pig-lead,
> Firewood, iron-ware, and cheap tin trays.

Look up

Abstract noun, Collective noun, Common noun, Compound word, Concrete noun, Countable noun, Pronoun, Proper noun, Uncountable noun.

Object

The object of a sentence is the thing being acted upon.

 Jenny threw *the ball*.

Direct and indirect object
'The ball' in the sentence above is sometimes known as the direct object, since it is the thing that has been thrown. The person or thing that receives the ball is called the indirect object.

 Jenny threw Ian the ball.

In this sentence, 'the ball' is the direct object, and 'Ian' is the indirect object, as he received the ball. Jenny did not throw Ian!

Look up
Direct object, Indirect object.

Old English

See English.

Participle

A participle is a non-finite form of the verb which allows the verb to be used as an adjective, and helps the verb form different tenses and voices.

Present and past
There are two participles, the present participle and the past participle.
- The present participle is formed by adding '-ing' to the base form of regular verbs.

  Eg. need → needing
  help → helping

- The past participle is formed by adding '-ed' or '-d' to the base form.

  Eg. need → needed
  blame → blamed

Look up
Non-finite verb, Past participle, Present participle.

Passive voice

When a sentence is in the passive voice, the subject of the sentence is acted upon by the verb.

Eg. Salt is added.
The criminal was arrested.

How the passive is formed
Passive constructions consist of a form of the verb 'be' and a past participle.

Eg. The message was received.
Buttonholes will be worn.
Dinner is served.

When the passive is used

The passive voice is most appropriate when the thing being acted upon is of greatest interest (rather than the doer of the action, for example), and for this reason it is very common in such things as the descriptions of science experiments.

 The water was heated, *rather than* I heated up the water.

The passive is also used when the doer of the action is actually unknown.

 The car was stolen.
Fire was discovered.

The passive is also useful when avoiding responsibility.

 The vase was broken, *rather than* I broke the vase.

Using the passive

The passive is often used in impersonal styles of writing.

 Guests *are asked* to leave their rooms tidy.
All applicants *are required* to fill in Form A37.

Long strings of sentences written in such a style can be confusing, and in general people find sentences written in the active voice easier to understand.

 You should leave your room tidy.
You must fill in Form A37.

Overuse of the passive voice is now frowned upon and there are campaigns throughout the English-speaking world to try to persuade officials to write clearer, active sentences. Some 'grammar checkers' in word processing software even warn you when you have used a passive construction.

85

 **Look up**

Active voice, Be, Past participle.

Past participle

The past participle is the form of a verb used with 'have' to describe a completed action, though not always in the past.

 You will have *finished* that by tomorrow.

How the past participle is formed

In regular verbs the past participle is formed by adding '-ed' or '-d' to the base form.

 worked, learned, wiped, hoped, heard

Irregular verbs use a variety of methods to form the past participle.

 lose → lost
know → known
see → seen
cut → cut
buy → bought

Uses of the past participle

- The past participle is used to form the 'perfect' tenses of verbs.

   I have *talked*   (*present perfect tense*)
  She had *lost*   (*past perfect tense*)
  We shall have *travelled*   (*future perfect tense*)

- When a verb is used as an adjective, it is often in the form of the past participle.

   a *known* quantity, *lost* property, a *broken* promise

- The past participle is also used with 'be' to form the passive voice.

   The door was *locked*.

 Look up

Adjective, Be, Irregular, Participle, Passive voice, Verb.

Past tense

See Tense.

Person

A verb is in the first, second or third person, depending on the noun or pronoun that is attached to it.

Which person?
- If the action of the verb is performed by the speaker or speakers, it is in the first person.

     I went to the cinema.
    We ate together afterwards.

- If the action of the verb is performed by the person or people addressed, it is in the second person.

     You are my only son.
    You all got the wrong answer.

- If the action of the verb is performed by something or someone else, it is in the third person.

     She is my best friend.
    They always play football on Saturday.

Third person singular
With the exception of highly irregular verbs such as 'be', only the third person singular of most verbs changes its form by adding an 's' when it is in the present tense.

     I run, you run, she *runs*

Narrative
The labels 'first person' and 'third person' are now most commonly used when talking about storytelling or narrative.
- A first person narrative uses 'I' as the main pronoun.

     I went to see my friends …

In a first person narrative, the writer or narrator is one of the characters in the story, and tells the stort from their viewpoint.
- A third person narrative uses 'he', 'she', or 'it'.

     She went to see her friends …

In a third person narrative, the writer or narrator describes events from an outside viewpoint.

- A second person narrative uses 'you'. This kind of narrative is not common.

     You went to see your friends …

 Reading activity

Read 'Complicity' by Iain Banks, or 'If on a Winter's Night a Traveller' by Italo Calvino. Why do you think the author uses second person narrative? Is it effective?

 Look up

Conjugation, Verb.

Personal pronoun

Personal pronouns are words that take the place of nouns. They are:

	Person	Subject	Object
Singular	1st	I	me
	2nd	you	you
	3rd	he, she, it	him, her, it
Plural	1st	we	us
	2nd	you	you
	3rd	they	them

 Look up

Pronoun.

Phrasal verbs

Phrasal verbs are verbs that consist of more than one word.

 Get on, put off, come about

How phrasal verbs are formed

Most verbs consist of a single word, but some very common ones, such as 'do', 'come', 'put', 'get' and 'go', change their meaning when a preposition or adverb is added.

Most phrasal verbs consist of two parts, but others have three. Compare 'put up a guest' and 'put up with a guest'.

put up a guest

put up with a guest

Look up

Adverb, Phrase, Preposition, Verb.

Phrase

A phrase is a group of words that forms part of a sentence.

Phrases and sentences

A phrase does not make sense on its own; it only makes full sense as part of a sentence.

When sentences are split into their component parts such as nouns, adjective, verbs etc., these parts may consist of more than one word. It is therefore more accurate to talk about noun phrases, adjective phrases and verb phrases.

Eg. <u>All my friends</u> <u>have been revising</u> <u>very hard</u>.
      noun phrase   verb phrase   adverb phrase

Look up

Sentence.

Plural

Words that refer to more than one thing are plural. Most nouns, pronouns and verbs have plural forms.

Look up

Noun, Singular.

Portmanteau word

See Word origins.

Possessive determiner

Possessive determiners, also known as possessive adjectives, precede nouns to show ownership. The possessive determiners are:

my, your, his, her, its, our, their.

Its

The most troublesome possessive determiner is 'its'. Because it is to do with possession, some people add an apostrophe (it's) as the apostrophe is also associated with possession. This is a mistake.

Look up

Apostrophe.

Possessive pronouns

Possessive pronouns are words that show who or what something belongs to. They are:

(singular)   mine, yours, hers, his, its
(plural)   ours, yours, theirs.

Look up

Pronoun.

Predicate

The predicate is what is said about the subject of a sentence.

Subject and predicate

Traditional grammars divided sentences into two parts, the subject and the predicate.

 <u>Donna</u> <u>lives in Cornwall</u>.

| Subject | | Predicate |

<u>The fire</u> <u>went out</u>.

| Subject | Predicate |

This division is seldom used in modern grammars because the subject is not always what the sentence is about, for instance in sentences with false subjects (e.g. 'There is a cat in the room').

False subject, Subject.

Prefix

A prefix is a group of letters that can be added to the beginning of a word to change its meaning.

 anti-, dis-, extra-, in-, micro-, re-, un-

Words that can have prefixes

Prefixes can be added to:

- nouns

    disagreement, extraterrestrial, microfilm

- adjectives

    inconvenient, immortal, unofficial

- verbs

    restart, demystify, unhook

- and to some adverbs

    unhappily, unenthusiastically.

The meaning of prefixes

Many prefixes give words an opposite meaning.

    de-, dis-, im-, un-

A
B
C
D
E
F
G
H
I
J
K
L
M
N
O
P
Q
R
S
T
U
V
W
X
Y
Z

Other prefixes have particular meanings that modify the base word.

 auto-, inter-, mega-

Knowledge of the meanings of these kinds of suffixes can help you to understand unfamiliar words.

 Look up

Affix, Suffix.

Preposition

Prepositions are words that show how one thing is related to another.

 above the fireplace
below the picture
with Harry

Even Prime Ministers Get it Wrong

ANOTHER lamentable piece of snobbery has been directed against our nice Prime Minister [John Major]. During his overwhelmingly impressive interview with Jeremy Paxman on Wednesday's Newsnight, it was asked what he would do if Labour won the election. He replied: "If is a very big preposition." It was not long before the Left-wing snobs like my Lord Jenkins of Hillhead, [and] Tony Blair ... were laughing themselves silly at this grammatical solecism.

'Pre', they said pompously, means before and 'position' means, well – er, 'position'. A preposition is word like 'of', 'in', 'on' or 'at' which qualifies a noun and is positioned before it in sentences. 'If' is a conjunction. It is all very well for someone of ancient lineage, like Lord Jenkins, who went to Eton and learnt Latin at his nanny's knee, to lampoon our Prime Minister's lack of education. But why can't they give the poor man a break? In loyalty to Mr Major, I shall in future treat 'if' as a preposition. 'And' is a noun. 'Yellow' is a participle. 'Although' is an adjective. Oh, yes.

A.N. Wilson, *Evening Standard*, 7 March 1997

(Even well-known writers get it wrong, too: prepositions never 'qualify' nouns, despite what Mr Wilson says!)

Prescriptive grammar

Prescriptive grammar bases its rules on how 'the best' speakers and writers use language, and derives a set of rules from this. Prescriptive grammarians comment on how language ought to be used, rather than on how it is actually used.

 Look up

Descriptive grammar, Grammar.

Present participle

The present participle is the '-ing' form of regular verbs. It is used in verb tenses, and when verbs are used as adjectives.

 I am *listening* to the speaking clock

How the present participle is formed
The present participle is formed by adding '-ing' to the base form of the verb.

  work → working
play → playing
pray → praying

Uses of the present participle
- The present participle is used to form the 'continuous' tenses of verbs.

 They are *watching*   (continuous present tense)
You will be *going*   (continuous future tense)
I have been *writing*   (continuous present perfect tense)
She had been *failing*   (continuous past perfect tense)
We shall have been
    travelling   (continuous future perfect tense)

- When a verb is used as an adjective, it is often in the form of the present participle.

  Eg. a *knowing* look, a *working* lunch, the *speaking* clock

Look up
Base form, Participle.

Pronoun

Pronouns are a class of words that are used in sentences to replace other parts of speech such as nouns, noun phrases or clauses.

Types of pronoun
Pronouns can be divided into several groups.
- personal: I, me, you, he, him, she, her, it, we, us, they, them
- possessive: mine, yours, his, her, its, ours, theirs
- reflexive: myself, yourself, himself, herself, itself, ourselves, yourselves, themselves
- demonstrative: this, that, these, those
- relative: who, whom, whose, which, that
- interrogative: who, whom, whose, what, which, whoever, whichever, whatever

Look up
Demonstrative pronoun, Interrogative pronoun, Personal pronoun, Possessive pronoun, Reflexive pronoun, Relative pronoun.

Proper noun

Proper nouns are the names of particular persons, places or things.

Features of poper nouns
You cannot normally use 'a', 'an', or 'some' in front of proper nouns. They begin with a capital letter and do not usually have a plural form.

  Eg. James, London Bridge, Technicolor

Look up
Noun.

Punctuation

Punctuation involves using symbols other than the letters of the alphabet to give information about intonation and meaning. Punctuation marks work within words, clauses and sentences. Some have a grammatical function; others show such things as missing letters or where a pause in breathing is intended.

Look up

Apostrophe, Bracket, Colon, Comma, Dash, Exclamation mark, Full stop, Hyphen, Inverted comma, Question mark, Semi-colon.

The Importance of Correct Punctuation

If you want to write the letter on the left, make sure you don't punctuate it as in the letter on the right.

Dear John,

I want a man who knows what love is all about. You are generous, kind thoughtful. People who are not like you admit to being useless and inferior. You have ruined me for other men. I yearn for you. I have no feelings whatsoever when we're apart. I can be forever happy — will you let me be yours?

Gloria

Dear John,

I want a man who knows what love is. All about you are generous, kind thoughtful people, who are not like you. Admit to being useless and inferior. You have ruined me. For other men, I yearn. For you, I have no feelings whatsoever. When we're apart, I can be forever happy. Will you let me be?

Yours,
Gloria

From *Games Magazine*, 1984

Question

Questions are sentences which are usually designed to gain a response from the listener or reader. In older grammars questions are said to be in the interrogative mood.

Features of questions

Question sentences always end with a question mark. Many questions begin with question words such as 'who' or 'what'. Others use auxiliary verbs such as 'do'.

 Did you leave the door open?

Some questions involve the swapping round of the subject and the verb of a statement.

 You are leaving   (*statement*)
Are you leaving? (*question*)

Types of question

There are several types of question.

- Information questions usually begin with question words such as 'who', 'what', 'where', 'why', 'when' and 'how'.

   When are you leaving?

- Yes–no questions are asking for 'yes' or 'no' answers (though they may get 'maybe').

   Are you leaving?
  Do you play cricket?

- Either–or questions involve alternative posibilities.

   Should I stay or should I go?

- Echo questions ask for information to be repeated.

   You said what?

Indicating a question

In speech it is possible to make a statement into a question by raising the tone of your voice towards the end of the sentence.

 You are leaving now?

This is shown in writing by the simple use of a question mark at the end of the sentence.

Questions that don't require answers

Some sentences are in the form of questions but do not actually require a response from the reader or the listener. These types of questions include:

- exclamations:

    Eg. Isn't it lovely!

- rhetorical questions:

    Eg. How should I know?

Look up

Auxiliary verb, Mood, Question mark, Question tag.

Did you break my trainset?

Question mark

The question mark is a punctuation mark which looks like this **?** .

Why question marks are used
Question marks are used to indicate that a sentence is a question. Some questions are shown by the order of words in a sentence; others are in the form of statements, but they are made into questions by the addition of a question mark.

> **Eg.** Are you going out tonight?
> Hamed will be coming, won't he?
> Cara is late?

 Look up
Question.

Question tag

A question tag is a short addition to a statement which turns it into a question.

> **Eg.** You are going to the party   (*statement*)
> You are going to the party, *aren't you*?   (*question*)

How question tags are formed
The tag is formed by using parts of the auxiliary verbs 'be', 'have' or 'do', plus the appropriate pronoun. The pronoun always comes after the verb (and 'not', if used). Many dialects and varieties of English have a general, all purpose question tag, such as 'isn't it?' or 'innit?'

Modal verbs in question tags
If a modal verb is used in a sentence that ends in a question tag, the modal verb is also used in the tag.

> **Eg.** They *can* come to the party, *can't* they?
> I *shouldn't* have bought the red one, *should* I?

This rule also applies to 'be', 'have' and 'do'.

> **Eg.** Kevin *hasn't* got a coat, *has* he?
> Mai *is* on the train, *isn't* she?

When there is no other modal or auxiliary verb in the sentence then 'do' is used.

 The dog ate the cat food, didn't it?
Jonah never won a prize, did he?

Positive and negative question tags
After a negative statement the question tag is positive in form.

 Hasan hasn't been here all week, has he?
We never win, do we?

After a positive statement the question tag is usually negative.

 Shazia has forgotten her book, hasn't she?
Evelyn wears glasses, doesn't she?
We are going tomorrow, aren't we?

Positive statements can also have positive question tags.

 So you're leaving, are you?

Look up
Auxiliary verb, Modal verb, Pronoun, Question.

Quotation mark

See Inverted comma.

Reflexive pronoun

Reflexive pronouns are used when the subject and the object of a sentence refer to the same person or thing. They are:

myself, yourself, herself, himself, itself, ourselves, yourselves, themselves.

 Pull *yourselves* together!
The cat washed *itself* carefully.

Look up
Object, Pronoun, Subject.

Regular

Regular means following a rule or pattern.

Patterns of language
The task of a grammarian is to look for the rules and patterns of language. Some regular patterns in English can be found in the conjugations and tenses of verbs, and in the number (singular/plural) of nouns.

I look, you look, she/he/it looks,
    we look, you look, they look   (*conjugation*)
look, looking, looked   (*tense*)
hat, hats   (*number*)

Conjugation, Irregular, Number, Regular, Tense.

Relative clause

A relative clause is a type of clause which gives extra information about the noun phrase to which it belongs.

Relative clauses in action
In formal writing, relative clauses are usually introduced by a relative pronoun.

 My car, which is a Jaguar, is brand new.

In the sentence above, the main piece of information is 'My car is brand new.' The extra information, 'which is a Jaguar', has been added in the form of a relative clause. The relative clause here is introduced by the relative pronoun 'which'.

Non-defining relative clauses
If the extra information provided by the relative clause is not necessary for the understanding of the sentence, it is called a non-defining relative clause.

 Jonathan, who lives next door, dropped in to see us.

In this sentence, 'who lives next door' is a non-defining relative clause because it is not necessary for an understanding of the sentence. 'Jonathan dropped in to see us' makes sense on its own.

Defining relative clauses
If the extra information provided by the relative clause is necessary for the full understanding of the sentence, it is called a defining relative clause.

 The boy who lives next door dropped in to see us.

In this sentence, 'who lives next door' is a defining relative clause because it tells us which particular boy came to visit. The sentence does not make full sense if the clause is left out. (Although 'The boy dropped in to see us' makes grammatical sense, it is not clear who is meant without the relative clause.)

'Which' and 'that'

When referring to things, 'which' is generally used to introduce non-defining relative clauses, and 'that' is used to introduce defining relative clauses.

 Sarah's favourite picture, which was the
largest in the room, was by Van Gogh.   (*non-defining*)
Sarah stood by the picture that was
next to the window.   (*defining*)

How to spot non-defining relative clauses

If a relative clause can be omitted from the sentence without loss of meaning it is a non-defining relative clause. Non-defining relative clauses are also often separated from the main clause by commas (see examples above).

Look up

Clause, Main clause, Relative pronoun.

Relative pronoun

A relative pronoun introduces a relative clause. Relative pronouns include:

who, whom, whose, which, that

Relative and interrogative

Words such as 'who', 'whose' and 'which' can also be interrogative words, but in this case they introduce questions rather than relative clauses.

Look up

Interrogative pronoun, Pronoun, Relative clause.

Reported speech

Reported speech (also called indirect speech) is a way of recalling speech in which the words spoken are treated as if they were events in the past.

Direct and reported speech

In direct speech (in which the actual words used are quoted), all that the reporter has to do is make clear who is speaking and how the words were spoken. In reported speech, however, there is a change of point of view so that pronouns, adverbs of time and place and tenses need to be adjusted.

 'You should have been here yesterday!'
shouted Helena.   (*direct speech*)

Helena shouted as us and said that
we should have been there the day
before.   (*reported speech*)

Ambiguous pronouns in reported speech

In reported speech it is often necessary to substitute third person pronouns for first person pronouns (e.g. 'he' or 'she' for 'I'). This can lead to ambiguity and confusion.

 Katrina said, 'I'll give her my return
ticket.'   (*direct speech*)

Katrina said that she would give her
her return ticket.   (*reported speech*)

In such cases the names of the person or thing referred to can replace the original pronoun. It may also be necessary to specify who a pronoun refers to in brackets.

 Katrina said that she would give Jane her (Katrina's)
return ticket.

Using reported speech

In writing, reported speech is used when the actual words spoken are not important or when the details cannot be recalled accurately. It is also used when the writer does not wish to slow the story down with a full-scale conversation.

 Reading activity

Reported and direct speech can often be used together to add variety to dialogue, for instance in the following passage from *Pride and Prejudice*.

> 'My dear Mr Bennet,' said his lady to him one day, 'have you heard that Netherfield Park is let at last?'
>
> Mr Bennet replied that he had not.
>
> 'But it is,' returned she; 'for Mrs Long has just been here, and she told me all about it.'
>
> Mr Bennet made no reply.

Here Jane Austen is able to foreground Mrs Bennet's talkativeness and suggest Mr Bennet's lack of enthusiasm for the topic of conversation.

Look up

Direct speech, Pronoun.

Reporting clause

A reporting clause is a clause used to show who is speaking and/or the manner of speech.

> **Eg** he asked, I said, she answered, they grumbled

Using reporting clauses

In your writing it is a good idea to make sure that there is plenty of variety in the reporting clauses. Your readers need information about how words were spoken as well as who was saying them.

Look up

Clause, Direct speech, Reported speech.

Semi-colon

The semi-colon is a punctuation mark which looks like this **;** .

Uses of the semi-colon
The semi-colon is used to indicated a short pause in a sentence, between a comma and a colon in length.

 I was uncertain what to do next; I was new to the game.

The semi-colon in the sentence above is used to link two statements, but semi-colons are also used to separate items in a list when commas might be confusing.

 In the car were: Joseph, my friend; Max, my cousin; Ralph the dog; and finally, me.

Colon, Comma, Punctuation.

Sentence

A sentence is a group of words that makes sense.

Features of a sentence
Some sentences can be a single word, others can be a single clause, but most sentences consist of more than one word or clause. Almost all sentences contain a subject and a verb, and in writing they begin with a capital letter and end with a full stop.

Types of sentence
There are four main types of sentences.
- Simple sentences contain only one clause.

     Yolande went to the station.

- Compound sentences contain two or more clauses joined together with a conjunction such as 'and' or 'but'.

  Eg. Kevin lives in Liverpool and Maria lives in Bristol.

- Complex sentences contain two or more clauses: a main clause and at least one other subordinate clause.

  Eg. Danny likes coffee, although it keeps him awake at night.

- Special (or minor) sentences are sentences that make sense but do not follow all the rules that govern other sentences. For instance, they may lack a subject or a main verb.

  Eg. Stop!
  Hey, you!
  Nil by mouth.

Special Sentence

The problem with sentences

One of the basic concerns of grammar is how words combine together into sentences. Grammarians have found it difficult over the years to arrive at simple definition of what a sentence is, but most sentences contain at least one complete action or thought. Few young writers have trouble starting sentences but some do have problems knowing where to finish them.

Look up

Clause, Complex sentence, Compound sentence, Full stop, Simple sentence, Special sentence, Subject, Verb.

Simple sentence

A simple sentence is a sentence containing only one clause.

 Salma went to the zoo.

Clause, Sentence.

Singular

Words that refer to one thing are singular. Most nouns, pronouns and verbs have singular forms.

Look up

Noun, Plural.

Slang

Slang is non-standard English, usually deliberately so.

Features of slang

Slang is very informal and is often restricted in its use to a particular group of people or to a particular place. Like jargon, it helps groups of people to identify with each other and often to exclude outsiders. For this reason slang often changes when it becomes too widely known. Slang can often be very inventive and colourful but it tends to be short-lived.

Acceptable slang

Some slang terms from the past are now part of Standard English, though usually at the informal end of usage. Examples are 'wicked' in the sense of good, and 'hassle' meaning problems or vexation.

Look up

Informal language, Jargon, Standard English, Word origins.

Smiley

A smiley (or emoticon) is a combination of keyboard symbols used in e-mail or chat forums to show how the writer is feeling or to make it clear, for instance, that a message is a joke.

How smileys work

Viewed from the side, with the head on the left shoulder, smileys look like faces.

 :-) This means 'I'm happy to hear from you'; it is sometimes used after a sarcastic or joking statement.

:-(The frowning smiley means 'I'm unhappy'; it is sometimes used when the writer did not like the last message.

;-) The 'winkie' is used is used for tongue in cheek remarks, to avoid giving offence.

There are many others.

The purpose of smileys

Smileys have emerged because of the informal nature of e-mail and chat forums. Exchanges often take place rapidly and writers do not have time to think about the best way of expressing their meaning before sending their messages.

Netiquette.

Special sentence

A special sentence (or minor sentence) is a group of words that make sense but lack some of the generally recognised ingredients of a clause or sentence.

What's missing?

A 'full' sentence usually requires a subject and a finite verb, but special sentences either lack these or take the form of a subordinate clause.

 Help!
No Smoking
As if you didn't know!

Traditional grammars explained that the missing parts of these sentences were 'understood', so that 'Help!' was really a short form of 'Help me!'

Where special sentences are used
Special sentences are often found in commands, signs or instructions.

 Shut up!
Keep Left
Open the package carefully

They are also found in advertising, where they can have a striking effect.

 Just be. (Calvin Klein perfume advertisement)

 Look up
Directive, Sentence.

Speech mark

See Inverted comma.

Split infinitive

A split infinitive is formed by placing an adverb between 'to' and the base form of a verb.

 to boldly go, to quietly wait

To split or not to split?
People have been complaining about the use of split infinitives for almost two hundred years. Grammarians who thought that Latin should be the model for good English noticed that the infinitive was never split in Latin and therefore decided that it should not be split in English (although in Latin the infinitive is one word and therefore cannot be split).

Some writers of English now avoid splitting infinitives, but in doing so they miss out on a way of changing the emphasis of a phrase. Compare the difference between the famous opening to *Star Trek*, 'to boldly go where no man has gone before', with the more grammatically 'correct' versions:

to go boldly where no man has gone before
boldly to go where no man has gone before.

 Look up

Grammar, Infinitive.

Splitting

Splitting is a way of focusing attention on both parts of a normal sentence. You can split it into two parts using 'it', the verb 'to be' and 'that' or 'who.'

 It was the dog that bit the cat. (*rather than* The dog bit the cat.)

Standard English

Standard English is the language spoken and written by the majority of educated speakers of English. It is also the language used by newsreaders, textbook writers, broadsheet newspapers and many novels. It is one of the dialects of English.

 Look up

Dialect, English, Formal language, Grammar.

Subject

The subject of a sentence is the person or thing performing the action of the sentence. Most sentences include a subject.

 Lisa threw the ball.
The Moscow State Circus set up its tents here tonight.

 Look up

Object.

Subjunct

A subjunct is a type of adverb that has a subordinate role in relation to a clause or part of a clause.

 Historically, Warrington was part of Lancashire.
Please leave the room.

The functions of subjuncts
Subjuncts can express:
- a point of view

     Legally, he didn't have a leg to stand on.

- politeness

     Kindly remove the seal from the container.

- attitude

     Unfortunately, Jason was proved right in the end.

- intensity or qualification

     I knew her *slightly*.
    I *sort of* knew her.

Look up
Adverb, Clause.

Subjunctive

The subjunctive mood is used when the content of the clause is being doubted, supposed, suggested etc. rather than simply asserted as true.

 If *I were* you *I would* buy a larger
packet.   (*not* If I was …)
If *he were* to arrive tomorrow
he would be welcome.   (*not* If he was …)
It is requested that answers *be* written (*not* that answers
on one side of the paper only.   are written …)

Look up
Mood.

Subordinate clause

Subordinate clauses are clauses related to the main clause of a sentence, which either give us extra information or complete the main clause.

How subordinate clauses are used
In the sentence below:

Wherever you go, don't go in the forest

the clause 'Wherever you go' is said to be subordinate to the main clause because it widens the sense of the main clause. It cannot stand as a clause on its own.

Subordinating conjunctions
Subordinate clauses are often introduced by a subordinating conjunction.

 Mai has hated the food *since* the day she arrived.

Look up
Main clause, Subordinating conjunction.

Subordinating conjunction

Subordinating conjunctions are words that connect a subordinate clause to a main clause.

Categories of subordinating conjunction
Subordinating conjunctions can refer to different categories,

depending on how the two parts of the sentence are related. They can refer to:

- time

  Eg. after, as, before, since, until, when, while

- place

  Eg. where, wherever

- manner

  Eg. as, like, the way

- reason

  Eg. as, because, since

- result

  Eg. so that

- purpose

  Eg. in order to, so that, to

- concession

  Eg. although, though, while

- condition

  Eg. if, unless.

Why subordinating conjunctions are useful

Subordinating conjunctions help readers or listeners to understand the relationship between one part of a sentence and another. Think, for instance, of how you could express the meaning of the following sentence without a subordinating conjunction.

The train was delayed while it was being refuelled.

Look up

Conjunction, Subordinate clause.

Suffix

A suffix is a group of letters that can be added to the end of a word to change its meaning or alter its grammatical function.

 -able, -er, -est, -ful, -ly, -ward

Changing the meaning

Some suffixes change the meaning of the word they are attached to.

 book → booklet
kind → kindness
change → changeable
Marx → Marxism

Altering the function

Many suffixes alter the grammatical function of a word.

 Talk, talks, talking, talker
Long, longer, longest

 Look up

Affix, Prefix.

Superlative

When adjectives or adverbs are being used to compare, they can be in either the comparative or superlative form.

Superlative adjectives

To make the superlative form of most short adjectives you add '-est'.

 hot → hottest
long → longest

'Most' is used with longer adjectives.

 beautiful   most beautiful
childish   most childish

Superlative adverbs

'Most' is used with adverbs, whether they are long or short.

 rapidly   most rapidly
often   most often

There are a few exceptions, however. The superlative of 'fast', when used both as an adjective and as an adverb, is 'fastest'.

Irregular comparison

Some words have irregular comparative and superlative forms.

	Comparative	**Superlative**
good	better	best
bad	worse	worst
many	more	most
little	less	least

Look up

Adjective, Adverb, Comparative.

Synonym

If two or more words have roughly the same meaning they are called synonyms.

The thesaurus

English is very rich in synonyms, which means that it is possible to express precise degrees of meaning. Lists of synonyms are organised into a book called a thesaurus.

Look up

Thesaurus.

Syntax

Syntax is the study of how words are arranged in sentences. Along with morphology (the study of the structure of words), syntax is one of the main concerns of grammar.

Look up

Grammar, Sentence.

Tense

A verb's tense is usually defined by whether the verb refers to the past, the present or the future.

How verbs show their tense
The tense is reflected in the form of the verb. For instance:

Simple present	Present continuous	Simple past	Present perfect	Future
I joke	I am joking	I joked	I have joked	I will joke
I am	I am being	I was	I have been	I will be
I see	I am seeing	I saw	I have seen	I will see

Watch out!
However, because a verb is in the present tense it does not necessarily refer to the present; think, for instance, of a newspaper headline such as 'England lose to Argentina'. Likewise, a sentence beginning 'If she arrived tomorrow ...' does not refer to the past.

Using tenses in narrative

In storytelling, writers have to decide whether to tell their stories in either the present or the past tense. Most stories are told in the past tense as if they have already taken place. Some stories are told in the present tense, which has the advantage of making the events appear to happen as we read. It is important not to mix the two storytelling tenses in the same stretch of narrative.

 Reading activity

Read *Everyone Else's Parents Said Yes*, or another of Paula Danziger's many books, and compare her use of present tense narrative with that of another author, such as Judy Blome.

Be, Have, Verb.

The

'The' (sometimes called 'the definite article') is used in front of nouns or noun phrases for various reasons.

Functions of 'the'

We use 'the':

- when the thing being referred to has just been mentioned.

    Eg. I picked up a pencil. I put *the* pencil in my pocket.

- when the thing referred to is unique or assumed to be familiar.

    Eg. Jenna visited the Empire State Building (*there is only one*)
    Are you going to the park? (*the speaker knows which one*)

- when the speaker or writer wishes to emphasise the uniqueness of a particular noun.

    Eg. Trafalgar Square is *the* place to be on New Year's Eve.

A, Noun.

Thesaurus

A thesaurus is a book containing lists of words which are similar or opposite in meaning. The purpose of a thesaurus is to increase the variety of language that you use, but if the grammatical information it provides is ignored it can lead to inappropriate choices.

The headword. This is the word that usually needs to be replaced in the user's writing

fan[1] *v.* **1.** *Often fig.* add fuel to the flames, agitate, arouse, enkindle, excite, impassion, increase, provoke, rouse, stimulate, stir up, whip up, work up **2.** air-condition, air-cool, blow, cool, refresh, ventilate, winnow (*Rare*) *-n.* **3.** air conditioner, blade, blower, propeller, punkah (*In India*), vane, ventilator

Synonyms, or words that have similar meanings to the headword.

Part of speech. This should be the same as the word being replaced.

Usage label. Make sure that the new word fits in with the style in which your are writing.

fan[2] adherent, admirer, aficionado, buff (*Inf.*), devotee, enthusiast, fiend (Inf.), follower, freak (*Sl.*), groupie (*Sl.*), lover, rooter (*U.S.*) supporter, zealot

Language variety label.

Antonyms antagonist, enemy, foe, opponent

Antonyms, or words with the opposite meaning to some senses of the headword

An extract from *The Collins Paperback Thesaurus in A–Z Form*

Look up

Synonym.

Transcript

A transcript is an exact writing down of speech which includes all the noises that the speaker makes besides his or her words.

Difficulties in transcription

Unfortunately for English spellers there are around 44 distinct sounds or 'phonemes' in English and only 26 letters available to represent them. Transcripts therefore often make use of a phonetic alphabet to write down speech accurately.

I'm	OK,	thank	you.	**Key**		
aɪm	əʊkeɪ,	θæŋk	jʊ	aɪ	*as in*	dive, cry
				m	*as in*	mat, mop
				əʊ	*as in*	note, phone
				k	*as in*	king, kill
				eɪ	*as in*	say, main
				θ	*as in*	thin, three
				æ	*as in*	act, mass
				ŋ	*as in*	sing, long
				j	*as in*	yellow, yes
				ʊ	*as in*	could, stood

A sentence transcribed in the phonetic alphabet, with a key to the pronunciation

Using transcripts

Transcripts are used to analyse how speech actually works, as opposed to how people think it works. Many people are under the impression that speech is like dialogue in films or plays, but transcripts of recordings of live speech show, among other things, that many sentences are unfinished, that speakers don't keep to a topic and that there are many interruptions and hesitations.

Grammarians use transcripts to discover the rules of conversational English, but they are also used in law courts, in parliament and in some types of therapy.

Look up

Direct speech.

Transitive verb

Transitive verbs are verbs that can take a direct object.

Eg. open, find, make, compare

Transitive and intransitive

Some verbs have both intransitive and transitive uses.

Eg. Magnus made for the car. (*intransitive*)
Leo made a sketch. (*transitive*)

'Lay' and 'lie'

The most common problem caused by the transitive and intransitive uses of verbs is with the verbs 'lay' and 'lie'. In Standard English 'lay' is usually transitive and 'lie' is intransitive.

Eg. Hens lay eggs.
You lie down here.

The second sentence should not be 'You lay down here.' The problem is made worse by the fact that the past tense of 'lie' is 'lay'.

I lay the table. (*present tense of 'lay'*)
The cards lay on the table. (*past tense of 'lie'*)

 Look up

Direct object, Intransitive verb.

Uncountable noun

Most types of nouns can divided into countable or uncountable categories. You cannot use 'a' or 'an' with uncountable nouns, but they can be preceded by 'some'. They have no plural form.

 luck, water, gold, butter, information

Grass is an uncountable noun.

 Look up

Countable noun, Noun.

Verb

Verbs are words that describe actions.

How verbs change their form
Verbs change their form according to their tense and the person (such as 'I' or 'he') that is attached to them. Regular verbs have four basic forms.

talk   (*the base form*)
talks   (*the third person singular form*)
talking   (*the present participle*)
talked   (*the past participle*)

Irregular verbs sometimes have varied or extra forms.

be: am, are, is, was, been
see: saw, seen
know: knew, known
speak: spoke, spoken
hit: hitting

Mood and voice
Verbs are either in the indicative, imperative, interrogative or subjunctive mood. They are also either in the active or passive voice.

Transitive, intransitive and copula verbs
Verbs can be transitive or intransitive, depending on whether or not they take a direct object. They are copula if they link a subject of the sentence with the complement.

Lexical, auxiliary and modal verbs
The majority of verbs describing actions are known as lexical verbs.

eat, run, listen, mutate, plot

The verbs 'be', 'have' and 'do' are known as auxiliary verbs, as they help other verbs to form their tenses or to form questions. These three verbs can also work as main verbs in a sentence.

Verbs such as 'can', 'may' and 'should' are known as modal verbs or modal auxiliaries. They help to modify the meaning of the verbs to which they are attached.

Using verbs

Verbs are key parts of the majority of sentences. Along with nouns they form the backbone of communication and need to be chosen carefully if writing is to be clear and accurate.

Look up

Active voice, Auxiliary verb, Copula verb, Intransitive verb, Modal verb, Mood, Passive voice, Person, Tense, Transitive verb.

Vocabulary

The vocabulary is all the words in the language.

Measuring the English vocabulary

It is often said that English has a very large vocabulary compared to other languages, but it is very difficult to say exactly how large it is. For instance, is 'chair' meaning a piece of furniture and 'chair' meaning the person in charge of a meeting one word or two? Do all the forms of a verb count as separate words?

Dictionaries

The number of 'headwords' in dictionaries gives some indication of the size of the English vocabulary – the *Oxford English Dictionary* lists over 200,000 words plus around 10,000 derivative words (for example, ending in '-ly' or '-ness'). Of these words about half are nouns, a quarter adjectives and about a seventh verbs. *Merriam-Websters Third International Dictionary*, an American dictionary, lists 450,000 words.

Individual vocabularies

As well as the whole vocabulary of English, there are individual vocabularies. These are usually divided into active vocabularies

A B C D E F G H I J K L M N O P Q R S T U V W X Y Z

(the words we use) and receptive vocabularies (the words we can understand). Receptive vocabularies are larger than active vocabularies because we can understand more words than we can actually use with confidence.

Vocabulary growth

One estimate of the size of an individual's vocabulary at different ages is:

9 year old	6,000 words
18 year old	18,000 words
college graduate	24,000 words
educated professional	30,000 words
Shakespeare	31,500 words

9 YEARS   **18 YEARS**

English, Word origins.

Voice

The voice of a verb can be either active or passive.

> 'B' team won the match.   (*active voice*)
> The match was won by 'B' team. (*passive voice*)

Active voice, Passive voice.

Word

The word is the most basic unit of meaning in speech or writing. Words can be combined to form phrases, clauses and sentences.

Look up
Clause, Phrase, Sentence.

Word origins

Where words come from
The question of where English words come from is a complex one. Some words are made up, some are inherited, in changed forms, from the very earliest languages, others are borrowed from foreign languages and some are made from existing elements of English.

The Indo-European language
If you go back far enough you could say that some of the words in English are derived from the ancient Indo-European language. Linguists have traced words and word combinations back to this language, which must have been spoken by our ancestors about five thousand years ago. There are no written records of the Indo-European language, but there are enough similarities between the languages of the Indo-European 'family' to suggest some of its ingredients.

Coining
At some point, however, all words must have been 'made up'. This process has continued throughout history so that many words have no known origins. For instance 'dog' appeared in the Middle Ages, replacing the Old English 'hund', but its precise origin is obscure.

New words are often coined to describe new things, or new situations.

 CD-ROM, guillotine, quark, pollster, commuter

Slang has often been the source of words that have now become respectable. For instance, the word yob was originally back slang for boy. OK?

On many occasions, new things are given the names of their inventor or promoter, or of a famous incident that happened at the time they emerged.

sandwich	(*named after the Earl of Sandwich*)
hoover	(*an early brand of vacuum cleaner*)
balaclava	(*named after a famous battle*)
bikini	(*appeared at the same time as an atom bomb test on Bikini Atoll*)

This kind of naming is particularly common in science where discoverers or inventors are honoured by having, say, a plant species, a new comet or a unit of measurement named after them.

📖 **Reading activity**

Use an encyclopaedia to find out who the following scientific units were named after.

Watt   Ohm   Farad   Hertz   Ohm   Volt   Ampere
Coulomb   Kelvin   Curie   Newton   Joule

Clipping

Some words are formed from the reduction of other words. Some of these are informal forms of the longer words, whilst other clipped words have replaced the longer forms.

Long form	Clipped form
Advertisement	Ad
Aeroplane	Plane
Examination	Exam
Facsimile	Fax
Influenza	Flu
Refrigerator	Fridge
Omnibus	Bus
Telephone	Phone

The above words show that clipped forms can be taken from either the beginning, the middle or the end of the longer forms.

When a word is newly clipped an apostrophe is sometimes used to show that letters are missing, but these are soon dropped when the word has passed into common use.

 'phone, 'plane

Portmanteau words

Sometimes a new word is formed by the running together of two words to make a new word. These are called portmanteau words, or blends.

 net + etiquette = netiquette (a system of rules for politeness on the Internet)
breakfast + lunch = brunch (a late breakfast or early lunch)
smoke + fog = smog (a form of air pollution)

Affixes

One of the most productive ways of extending the meaning of a word is by adding prefixes and suffixes to existing words. Some suffixes, such as -ing and -ed, are to do with the grammatical function of a word, but others, such as -ism or -er, change their meaning.

 read: reading, reader, readable
Marx: Marxist, Marxism
care: careless, carelessness, carelessly, careful, carefree

Prefixes are equally productive of new words.

 read: reread, misread, unread
place: replace, misplace, displace

📖 *Reading activity*

How many prefixes and suffixes can you count in the following words?

Antidisestablishmentarianism
Unreconstructed
Misinformation
Disinterestedly
Polychromatism

Back formations

Some words, such as 'editor' or 'baby-sitter', arrive in English in one form which then gives rise to other uses such as 'edit' or 'baby-sit'. This process is known as 'back formation'. There are many examples of this process.

```
beggar → beg
burglar → burgle
difficulty → difficult
double-glazing → double-glaze
lazy → laze
television → televise
```

Meaning change over time

The meaning of words is not static, and with the passage of time some words undergo quite large shifts of meaning. For instance, the word 'manufacture' originally had the sense of 'made by hand', whereas today it tends to mean 'made by a machine'. The word 'saelig' in Old English means 'holy'; its modern descendant is 'silly'.

Such shifts in meaning can cause difficulties when reading older works of literature. Below are some examples of words and what they probably meant to older authors.

Word	Modern meaning	Author	Author's meaning
Nice	pleasant	Jane Austen	precise, exact
Girl	a young female	Geoffrey Chaucer	any young person
Awful	very bad	John Milton	inspiring awe
Anon	eventually, soon (as in 'see you anon')	William Shakespeare	immediately

Look up

Affix, Compound word, English, Morphology, Slang.